The Enchanted World of Twin Flame

Book One

By Sylvia

Twin Crows® Publishing House.
ISBN: 978-0-578-61370-3

Acknowledgements

I have many people I'd like to acknowledge and thank for their assistance in the making of my book and this book coming into existence.

The first person I'd like to give a wholehearted big shout out to is my Beautiful Divine Masculine. You have always been my Biggest Support, my First Love, my Muse in this journey and my Heart in this Mission. You truly are the most amazing person I know. I will always hold you with the highest regard and please remember that only Love is Real. This book could not have been written if we did not have the amazing experience we shared (as ironic as this may sound to you, you have been the one to keep me sane through all of it). You probably already know this, but I thought I'd take a moment to state the obvious: This book is our love story. It was written through extreme pain, but it was my desire to find solace for my heart that enabled me to finish this book and see it through. It would lend to the most painful journey of searching myself and my world to understand why our story had to play out in the way it did, but it was through the darkness and the pain that I found the light and the meaning of True Love. This is why I share our story, as it was the pain that taught me how to love unconditionally. And Love is the magic of Twin Flames and what keeps it all going. Our story is a story that has no end. May you always know my love for you is real. I Love You Eternally.

I thank my family for being patient with me on my journey of awakening. To my children, may you always know how special each of you are to me.

To all my fans, followers, and subscribers of my YouTube channel, "The Enchanted World of Twin Flame," and other media sites, thank you for the astounding support over the years.

To my closest friends on this journey, you know who you are individually. I send you love and light.

To Kim Cressell, my editor, friend and fellow Twin, a huge acknowledgement to you for all your tireless efforts in making this all come to fruition. Your perseverance and commitment to helping me accomplish my biggest dream and mission has been godsent. I don't think that "thank you" is a big enough phrase to express my gratitude, but please know that I am truly thankful for what you've done to assist me in completing this undertaking.

I'd like to thank Joshua Brown, who has assisted me on my mission with my creative artwork and projects. Specifically, on this book, he designed the creative scheme of many of the photos. I extend lots of gratitude to you for your talents and labor, and I am extremely grateful for your friendship and support over the years. To Dustin Christensen, thank you for your friendship and your financial assistance in my mission and this specific project. I'd also like to thank Chelsea Fone, the designer of the book's cover and jacket.

To all my friends and fellow Twins on the journey, a big shout out to each of you. I Love You All.

Sylvia

Table of Contents

Acknowledgements.. iii

Entangled Souls...1

The Connection 4

From the Beginning 8

The Bubble Phase: "Remembering" the Silver Lining of Love 14

The Illusion of Our Time...24

Remembering My Beloved, A Memory of a Distant Past:
    The Energy of Eve..31

The Door to Eden...35

Our Telepathic Connection is Born................................42

Nothing Else Mattered 47

Eternal Love 52

The Shadows..58

Trust 65

The Test 72

Storm of Emotions...81

The Roadmap to Unconditional Love 85

Push and Pull 93

God's Will...96

"I Don't Do Labels" 103

Cruel Intent 110

Mind Craft: Superhuman Abilities 117

The Spiritual Cross...124

London's Double-Edged Sword 130

The Artful Mind 138

Spiritual Warfare 150

When London Left 155

Reviews 169

About Sylvia...170

"As above, so below."
"As within, so without."

The Naked Truth

Entangled Souls

I'm going to share my story with you. It's an incredible, true story, one filled with thrilling highs and virtually bottomless lows. A story that combines the greatest ecstasy of human pleasure with the awe-inspiring knowledge of God, the Angels, and the spiritual realms—a place where pure, unconditional love really does exist. Yes, like the kind of love you would find in fairy tales, but even better. This is my story about a passion-fueled, unconditional love between me and my Beloved, a love I did not expect. A love that turned my ordinary world upside down in every conceivable way. This is a story of a hard-working, passionate nurse and entrepreneur who met a rugged, charming police officer-turned-business-owner in a string of events that forever changed our hearts, our paths, and our destinies.

This love between the two of us is a love that is felt on a different level, a connection of a different kind, the entanglement of two Twin souls. It is the ultimate union, the perfect connection, the complete relationship experience. It is the connection of the perfect balance of love, on all levels: the body, the mind, the heart, the spirit, and the soul. When I found my Twin Flame, a concept I had yet to learn the meaning of, I experienced a feeling that was on a different level of understanding. It was a relationship so intense that nothing, nor anyone, even came close. The impacts were extreme, and the highs felt from the connection multiplied 10-fold and were euphoric in nature. The lows carried the same intensity and were treacherous to endure. It was love in its most pure form, ecstasy, a sort of amplified bliss. This love story—so vigorously passionate—consumed every aspect of our reality.

We were pulled together by a magnetic force, a connection orchestrated by the heavens above. Divine intervention, which brought us together, would sustain the force and the romantic connection, as well as a strong sexual attraction. These alluring truths kept us transfixed at that moment in time.

My story, the story of London and me, is a story of true love, but not in the traditional way of understanding love. This love was different. It was God-sent. It was divine. It came from a different place, from the heart and how we all experience love, but it was much deeper. It was felt on an entirely different level, at the core of my being. It was pure, raw, natural affinity. It was unconditional, intoxicating, addictive, and with no boundaries and no limitations. In short, it was a fantasy I never even knew I had.

Transcendence is a key part of my story, my journey into the unknown. The mystical love affair between my Twin and I would lead us into places within our souls that we would both excavate to find answers. This love would test our values, our minds, our thoughts, our ideas, and our perceptions, and it would send us on an unparalleled journey of spiritual growth and understanding. It would propel us on a journey of soul searching and looking for answers to the most cryptic of clues.

This journey opened doors to the spiritual realm, a reality I never even knew existed. This journey would make me question everything that was ever real to me and, ultimately, it would give me an understanding of spirituality. In the end, I learned through all of it that I was chosen for this path of spiritual enlightenment, and this process of spiritual growth would take hold of my life and change me as a person in every conceivable way.

The journey and subsequent deep soul searching would result in me understanding my life's purpose and then, a spiritual awakening started to unfold. My Third Eye was activated, and many revelations occurred that illuminated the truths of my deepest secrets, insecurities, and self-proclamations. I now possessed an awareness of things from a different vantage point. I was now able to connect the natural to the supernatural, and true love to true relationships, as they all work together to formulate the perfect balance to oneness through the unity of divine love. Finding the perfect balance meant finding my truth, and that brought my soul harmony and the understanding that everything in life must come full circle in order to be complete.

The key to this harmony is the understanding that God and the universe are in control of all things and that we must trust God, the Creator, in every way. I was able to understand that God already had a plan for my life, that he had already written my book of life, and that He is the Alpha and the Omega, the beginning and the end. Trusting meant allowing God to be in control. Giving it all to God was what I had to do, but it was the most difficult thing I've ever done. It meant giving up complete control and allowing God to do His will. This also meant I would also have to accept the outcome without prejudice, as difficult as the outcome might be.

I was no longer living my own life, my own selfish existence. I now walked with a different purpose; it was no longer just my own. I was now on a spiritual walk, a journey of three embodied into one. I know now that this Twin Flame connection is for a higher purpose, a greater cause, and the cause is ultimately to assist in raising consciousness and to forge an awareness of spirituality in the earthly realm.

The Connection

The Twin Flame connection is an instant knowing or feeling of coming home; the concept of connection is what embodies this relationship. It is a connection felt in a gaze, a familiarity of the soul, a recognition of the mind, and an attraction of the heart because you already know this heart. It is a knowing the instant you first see this person and are in the presence of who they are. However, at the same time, you recognize and realize that although you've never seen nor met this person before, you know who they are. This connection, this journey, has yielded many insights and revelations, including the significance of the connection between our bodies, our minds, our hearts and our soul, the very essence of my story. This connection is the magic between London and me, but because it was such a strong connection, this would be the very thing that would make our relationship impossible.

Two energetic pulls brought us together by the forces of nature and divine intervention. My Twin Flame, literally my other half. When we connected, our souls were bound. With a Twin Flame union, there is a binding of the spine that intertwines both twins. Like a serpent of light energy that travels up the spine, it leaves its source of energy lingering in the mist of tincture. This light of a spiritual nature energizes the union and links the relationship from the core. This connection is eternal and can never be severed, nor broken. Our souls came together to tell a story of true love's beauty, its power, and how it was able to sustain us through space and time.

This union is (and was) so intense, it would take me to places in my mind that would test my sanity. My heart felt the magic of this union and it was filled with joy and exhilaration, but my mind would be tested to the brink of complete and total meltdowns and insanity. My mind lived somewhere between heaven and hell during this relationship; it was marked with emotions that were like a dynamic, living roller coaster that traveled between the darkness and light. The romance was so massively explosive, it was like a magnetic force that controlled its pull of energy. Love and madness, good and evil, heaven and hell, one was not one without the other.

We were two water signs who were brought together by the fire of a shooting star that allowed us to cross paths, but the energy felt was that of the pressure of water being vaporized by fire, which was the byproduct of our love. All the degrees of the effects of fire and water were manifested by the experience.

London and I found a fantasy world in this bond. We both felt the intensity, like a natural high, a feeling of euphoria. It was the coming together of a police officer and a nurse: One, a very masculine character and its opposite, its female counterpart, with equal parts push and pull. The yin and the yang, we embodied this concept in our personalities. The first, a masculine and arrogantly natured man. The second a sweet, soft-spoken gal, who is very feminine in nature. Both of our professions were a representation of who we were, but in common, we were entrepreneurs, and both of us had built businesses from our individual passions. Together we were a force of nature, through our combination of hard work and dedication, and all the while, we stayed true to who we were and our passion for life by giving back to and serving our communities through our work and professions.

The fantasy world we found together became our reality. We indulged in the moment, we sank into it, we dove, we fell...deep. We both felt the connection and it was profound until the intensity became our truth and the supernatural aspect of the union was too fervent. His presence was understood in my soul, but my mind had never experienced anything like it. Our sexual encounters were so raw, the emotions could only be explained as pure and natural, intoxicating and addictive.

Our minds did not comprehend the connection. It was no longer logical, and it became too hard to sustain. As this relationship began to show its true colors and our self-awareness rose, we began to question what this connection really was.

We searched our own souls that reflect on one another, with their pain and past hurts. As this happened, the experiences of the world upon us began to surface. We looked to one another for answers, but neither of us had answers, and neither of us comprehended what was happening. The more and more we got involved, the deeper and deeper this process pulled us from within. But the understanding of "why" was not revealed to us.

All our truths surfaced, and no secrets could be kept from the other. Our souls could look at one another and see mistruths. There were no lies because we reflect on the other and a mirror cannot change the truth that stands in its presence. Our eyes are, in fact, the windows to our soul and to look into London's eyes was to see any truth that lay in its existence. In fact, this experience when looking into London's eyes was that of looking straight into a mirror. It was a reflection of our truth and what was going on in the inside without holding anything back. No hiding, no parts or pieces, it was all there for the other to see, revealed to us through the mirror of the eyes; it was the naked truth.

Our story is a beautiful story of true love: A supernatural kind that represents God's love. This love was divine. It was so pure, it was intoxicating. It was so intoxicating, it was toxic. It was a love so natural; it was supernatural. This love possesses a magnetic force and it was like a radiating mystical power that came from the core of our being. It was a connection of the soul on a spiritual level. When we became more and more involved with one another, this soul connection would take on a different meaning.

We started to connect on the spiritual level, and our souls came together even more, though we didn't recognize what it was that we were doing at the time. We also started connecting on a different parallel. We were able to talk telepathically to one another and each meeting became a meeting of the minds connecting, coming together to send and receive messages from the other: It was our encoded gift of words for the other.

The most bewildering and beautiful part of the story is that once we crossed over, once we understood the connection for what it was, we could spiritually connect with the other whenever we wanted. We could find the other, communicate, and even be in the presence of the other half. I literally began to have an affair, a full-on relationship with London, on a spiritual level.

My Dearest Love,

Would you believe me if I told you there is a second part to our story?

Would you believe me if I told you my heart could never give up on you?

My heart always knew it wasn't over; it wasn't over for me!

Our beautiful story of true love's bliss; it isn't over!

Funny thing is, you once asked me, what I would call "us"? I look to you and answer, and I say "a relationship" because that was my only understanding of it. London, I say "a relationship" because words could not do it justice. There are no words, only a feeling and an understanding of the divine nature of its beauty.

My love, it took a book to answer your question and I dedicate this book to you and our love story.

From the Beginning

Our love story is of a complex nature, spiraling through time and space, and with many layers of understanding love. It is a type of love, in reverence to all the ages, the harmonics of Gem, the mind. Our love is made up of each other, for we are an artifact of our time. The combination of time and love followed the evolution of understanding of "our time," but "our time" is and was that of the spirals of time, the ripples of spiritual nature, a walk through the spheres and cones of transcended vibrations and yet, the stillness of it would render the true meaning of it all, for it was time, the essence that existed within ourselves of inner synchronization.[*]

One would need to understand sacred meaning and with that, the many layers of understanding of love. A gist in meaning, in the sacred union, as through sacred geometry would be some clues to this, in the element of the vibration of love. My words, and London's (to each other) would become our gift to the other of insights into the soul, a connection to our spiritual reality through the window of the eyes, the soul of contour.

The meaning of our words was an innuendo of a spoken dialect of two powerful minds: enchanted, engrossed, connecting, in a lingo of love, but love carries with it many meanings and embraces so many emotions. Emotions which included pleasure, lust, beauty, sorrow, and pain. This lingo of love is like music, of a chromatic nature, the

---

[*]   *Chroma is the Greek word for color and indicates <u>Chroma feature</u>, a quality of a <u>pitch class</u> which refers to the «color» of a musical pitch, which can be decomposed in into an octave-invariant value called «chroma» and a «pitch height» that indicates the octave the pitch is in Chroma meaning of a scale, interval, etc. involving only notes proper to the prevailing key without chromatic alteration; (of a melody or harmony) constructed from a diatonic scale*

scale of pitch. The octave, music notes in unison, with each pitch a semitone of a tuning system of equivalent temperament of sound. To play this music of love was like that of a Chroma embellishment of undertone. It encompassed these emotions of pleasure, a reflection of diatonic notes, each in accord with the nature of our words.

The emotions we feel are of a lustful nature, but like this music, each has an overtone with a vibration of passion, beauty, a strong sentiment of desire, and the counter: the ineffable quality of lust which with lust must become the result of it, that of an unorthodox outcome, for it was sorrow and pain that would soothe me in gist. As with intense love, the pleasures of strong desires and deep affection also lie the inborn grief of its alternative nature, its inherent ties to suffering.

It is a song of divine quality and tone, for divine intervention is that which transcends through us as we engender this combination of complex desires. This language of love and truth bonded us forever, for it was the sensation of this vibration of sound and the root of the song we played in harmony. Although still in discord, the thought of this lustful passion is the song and desire of the outcome. The undertone is that of the endless knot, the wheel of life, the melody we play together would be the golden ratio of sound. To stay in the Love Vibration would bring us to the scale of music; this frequency would be the key to understanding our new world.

London was my master teacher in person, then he became my master guide in spirit. Like an angel who was sent to me from the heavens as a gift, an orchestration of paramount proportions would take place, and this would change the scene of my life ever after. That key, the golden note of the elements of the dissolute come together as the purified nature of our love, but it would mean that, like an angel, he came to shine his light over me. It was through this illumination of light that I could see my life more clearly, for things that needed to be fixed and removed would be placed in front of me like the scent of a candle…its fragrance lingered, but then once it was burned away to nothing so were the things that no longer stayed, like ashes they were burned to seethe.* For it was through this burning away of the old that my life's purpose would emerge, and like the Phoenix, I would rise out of the ashes.

His words hummed with the vibration of attunement, so powerful in snare, they felt like a double-edged sword, a vault that riveted my soul. His words of accord would carry so many meanings and truths with my being, truths of an element of allure and thus, this allure to a different understanding of Gem, or the mind. My angel, my purest of the element of light, was like a shrine over me. In this light, it would come to pass of the messages being delivered. They were in a direct parallel with a precision that radiated within my heart and soul. Never were words so hard to hear, especially when they were deeply rooted and when they came from places where these truths were buried and wanted to be forgotten.

London came into my life, just like the whirlwind that he would be to my life; he was this, too, to every aspect of my being. As we were getting ready to meet on this lineage of time, my whole world was being transformed in preparation for him. Three days prior, as the winds of change were making our union possible, I ended a long-term relationship. As that relationship came to its natural end, I called out to London by way of the universe of knowledge and with that a vibration of harmonics heralded his coming, for it is now set forth and so is his presence in my world, as police intervention was needed—and a police officer who would change my life—suddenly crash-landed into my world.

The experience of our first meeting is so clearly delineated in my mind as I write this, because it was the first time I saw him. A moment in time captured like an image of light, a standing of time alone for the reflection in that moment was that of the stillness of all things. Everything stopped and started at the same moment, the tick of that second when our eyes met.

---

* *Seethe is an archaic word, no longer in common usage, meaning, "To cook (food) by boiling it in a liquid.*

I went for a jog on this particular morning on a trail up the street from my house called the Virginia Corridor Trail. I got to the corner of where my street meets the trail and I saw his patrol car as it was about to turn onto my street.

I looked and saw him for the first time. I knew that this officer was coming to my house, so when I looked over at him, I was instantly caught in his gaze. I turned around, only to notice that he had not taken his eyes off me, nor had I taken my eyes off him. He was at a stop, but then he continued to drive very slowly, but his eyes did not leave mine until he drove past. I ran home, because I didn't want to miss him. When I got there, he was already inside the house talking to my son. The instant we were in the other's presence, we were mesmerized in the moment, but we both didn't know what to make of it. We tried to ignore it, this familiarity, and we almost dismissed it, but it was distracting and had both of our attention.

I introduced myself and invited him to my kitchen and I asked him to sit down. I offered a cup of coffee and he declined. This is a funny side note, but coffee would become a big part of our story, a part of our connection to the natural world. I went ahead and poured myself a cup and looked down at my hands. I noticed that my hands were shaking, and he noticed this, too.

I looked up at him and noticed the way he was looking at me, studying me and really taking me in. I was wondering if this was part of his job to do this, but I was thinking it's something else. I began talking and told my story. Immediately, I liked the way he listened, and I had his full attention. He was easy to talk to and he was an attentive listener. This was intriguing to me. He was listening without any interruption.

I started to go off course a little to test him. I wanted to know if he was going to cut me off, but he didn't. He didn't even get distracted by it; he just kept taking in my words. When he sensed I was about to finish with my account of what had happened, he abruptly stood up and leaned against the kitchen sink. I paused for a second and I

11

looked over at him and I noticed how he was just taking me in with his eyes.

I was trying to stay focused on what I was saying, but I couldn't help but notice the way he was looking at me. I had to stop talking mid-sentence and look up at him, and we just stared into each other's eyes. We both felt something. It was this familiarity of the other, but it was hard to understand because we were meeting for the first time. I picked up and finished my thought and now, it was his turn.

He acknowledged the shift in conversation with a nod; he had cordially given me my time to talk and now it was his turn. He did something interesting: He reached across his chest, up to his police camera, and he turned it off. He intently looked me in the eye and cut through all the B.S. and said, "I want to help you because you are being bullied and I was once in your shoes." He got personal with me and told me a little about his personal situation. I was taken aback by him, initially because he was genuine and sincere, a couple of qualities that I fancy in a person, and secondly, he was telling me about such a personal matter and trusting me with this information.

He mentioned that I would most likely need legal counsel and that I could at least call and get some guidance for how to move forward. He offered me his business card and told me that his personal phone number was on the card. He went on to say that I could call him when he was off work and he could give me some contact information for one of the best attorneys in town. In my mind, I was wondering if he liked me and was trying to ask me out, or if he was really wanting to reach out to just help me out.

I'm intrigued and I wanted to know, so I wait until it is "later," and I text: "Hi, London, thanks for taking the time to listen to me and my story! I appreciate how intently you listened to what I had to say and secondly, that you offered to help me. By the way, are you a single man?" London answered back: "Single and yes, a man. Let me get you that information…"

And so, this was the beginning of our story, and the start of our journey into the unknown, a world we would discover together. Forces of nature that we did not yet understand were coming into place, and the energy that surrounded this meeting made way for the forces that brought us together.

The Bubble Phase: "Remembering" the Silver Lining of Love

The unveiling of our love would begin in the space of understanding the silver lining. This is a space where you can feel (the love is felt like it is borne on you), but there is an element of the unseen as if your sight is blurred. It felt, and feels still, like a concert of emotions playing out in the mind. It is like being in a dream state, or a sort of orchestra of the divine. This feeling was the "One" feeling that I could never forget or quite get accustomed to, for it had a shock value to it. Every time I was around London, his presence felt like a jolt of energy. It felt like this strange impression, something that affected my energy field and literally touched my soul. I started to sense something else at this time. It was like a mask was placed over our eyes…as this would be a different reality we were to embark upon, and it was to take in the experience and live the experience in order to understand what was happening to us.

We couldn't have known at this time what this was, but we were being prepared to grasp our connection and then the understanding would come after. It would come, yes, this was understood, but not for a long time and not in the way of our understanding. Instead, it would be an organic process and it was an unfolding of our love. It was our Awakening process of spiritual love; first it would come from all our senses, then be revealed and experienced in a very natural and gradual way. It started with a lustful nature, and then would turn into something very supernatural. In this short time of getting to know one another, a single word would sum up this experience— oneness—but it was to understand and experience oneness that would change the meaning of *everything* for me. The very perception of life and how I viewed it would change in the uncovering of our love.

As the unveiling of our love played out, it felt like a ritual of divine nature as I started to recognize this feeling of pure essence. It was like a vase of perfume being poured over our soul. One could sense the pleasure of its scent, a sweet aroma to every awareness of our being. It is an anointing, for his sweet scent was now imbued in all things conceived in me. The cosmic essence of the heart was poured over us. It is pure water of a holy nature, a full view of unruly emotions that showered over us. "All that is," held in the foreshadowing of the vase of the heavens and within it, the art of apothecary. For in this vase is the purified water of aroma turned to the fermented oil of myrrh, which materialized over us, in emotions, or one may venture to call this memories—sensations—so powerful that the impression was a like a rainbow ray of sentiments, felt on our subtle bodies, the primal nature of connection. The showering of the union would come with an array of symbolic nature, the element of a ray of light of every hue that would touch us with a harmonious vibration of Gem (the mind); it is a different tone of the soul, of which is its true substance.

My perception could only fathom the knowing that he was "The One," as this story is that of the one, the one true love, the greatest of all loves. But to understand who he genuinely was to me would be the meaning of the book itself. "The One." What did that mean? For it was to take in the inference and let the undertone of that word take meaning to the heartstrings, the heart's key tone. First, I must open my mind to the bewilderment of the attunement of love to my heart, as our love was a lesson of music, a note of the soul. My memories take me to the dense reality of our time, as the memories leave the impression of fondness of his character, that of a kindred spirit of heart. To interpret his character to the countess of emotions, for the emotions acquired over me would be to explain Jasper, the philosopher's stone: the living spirit of love set forth to the mind, heart, and soul. The meeting of these elements regarded every affection, what was to articulate such muddled and contradictory feelings, as the senses were felt like a noose. This noose felt like it had taken ahold of my heart and was wrapped tightly around its walls, propelled by pure illusion and lust. The allure would be the byproduct of the union, a fixation of my heart. Consequently, this noose would be pulled by the grip of love's power over my soul and my mind, left to make out the twist and knots of the tempered tie of instinctive desire.

For the judgment of time would be the reverence of the paradox of this love. Decree, wisdom, insight, perplexity…the sharpness of the tongue…all the triggered sentiments of the passion and force of this love. The one love that would blindside me, as pain is the inferred experience when it is no more. It is the polarity effect that is extracted. The illusion would sustain the love that existed, as the fire smolders with smoke fumes as it fueled the impulse to understand this pain, as this pain was the mark of our separation. This was love: That was not in question, but this love was different. It was the one love that withstood time alone, for the elements rendered were the memories of the time in merging. It would be the origins of us and the foundation that would transmute to purify its form of matter, the source that ignites the flame.

What is this understanding, for to understand would be to let go of everything I knew? The cube and bubble that I lived in would ignite and explode, a combustion of truth. The patterns that made up this cube would shed some meaning as the patterns within lived the knowing of something that came from the truths within the mystical ties. As with this desire of innate nature came the underlying meaning to the tree of life…this was the wisdom of the soul. This tree of life would give meaning to the link between the spiritual and the human energy that lived inside of this cube, this link to the human and divine, for the secrets that lived in this esoteric space would be the creative energy within us, of a higher purpose in the promises and the visions that its fruit preserves life and its seed would be our fortress. Within this seed of creative nature was the energy of creation of the forces of sexual energy that existed in this bond. This energy would come with surges and halts. It would come with divine timing and without warning. It was an energy of the sacred power of outpouring, but the challenge would be to stabilize this energetic pull and achieving balance would be the greatest of all trials.

This would be the beginning of understanding, the pulling of all elements to figure out these challenges, but the other was to be physically present for all of it and to face these tests. These tests would awaken in us, as the emotional burden of this encounter would prove exhausting and daunting. The synchronization of this higher energy would be the focus of shifting our energy body and allowing a higher love to find us. What did this mean? In order to do this, I would have to "let go" and to "let go" would be to figure this out.

To understand this would be to first understand the concept of one or two, or you may say two of one. One was the magic world: As one, we were incarnate in two bodies in this time, but time was our illusion. In 3-D, the illusion of time would be to come together in spirit with that knowing. There was no separation of time, for time is only that of appearance. But I fought this, as my battle becomes one of love's power. I don't want to let go of this love. This love, this one true love, was my battle for it now consumed everything and was far more powerful than me. It expanded over everything and I fought for this love because it was my only choice, as this is was what I was compelled to do. It was the only thing my natural self would let me do and so with everything I knew, I would fight for this love between us. But to fight would also consume all of me. I knew I had to fight for this. It was not even a choice, but how would I fight? For this love was that of spirituality. This was nothing I knew and with that understanding, what did it mean to fight spiritually for love? This would be where I started my journey of love. It would be a configuration of the very understanding of love's powers, the golden refined metal, the sacred science of alchemy, the philosopher's stone, the transmutation of it all, for we are a mirror of higher spiritual transformation and the base is us.

This love of such complex nature and the power of its desires was that of pure lust of the heart. I came to find that for this type of love, I would have to let go of everything, for it meant I would have to surrender it all: my soul, my mind, and my heart would be left with the pure element of Jasper and the raw, benevolent longing for only refinement would lead to its facet of all.

But to surrender. How would I surrender, as I had to understand the nature of this love? For this love was of a different kind and it would mean I would have to sacrifice, and sacrifice would be the key to deliverance. But to deliver myself would be to deliver to the only element that was left in the mist of all of it, the fire of the illumination of love. It was the radiance of the divine, it was the brilliance of its ray of light, and the heat of its passion. The passion would be the force and with that force, the enlightening of the essence of the spirit, for the spirit was in fact the coming back to the one, for with that, this "one love" carried the compound of true love's essence, the essence of it all. This was the one source, the connection to it all: the soul. The soul level of love is based on an energetic whole and this would be the secret to figuring out this circle in which we rotated.

Where to start? To start at the beginning would be to start at the end, like the serpent that bites its tail, full circle. So instead, I will start in the middle, the point of zero, or zero point. My story is with the same complexity of understanding this zero point, for this is where I meet my Beloved. It was in my memory of this realm the most marveled upon events of this life, as it was to remember my love and to live this moment of time with him in the physical world of illusion. The dense cavity of this world would only allow our expression of love to be seen, but it was with the eyes of the soul that we would understand the obscurity of nature in its natural elements. For this was "in time," the time I got to spend with my London. It was in the physical, but the physical was our understanding of our time in the present, but our time is not based on the present, for it was at a crossroad of the lineage of time that we met, but nonetheless, I will start at this lineage.

It was a time of getting to know him and his essence, that which was the extracted identity of his soul. Truly, this was a fascinating time… London was everything my mind could ascertain that it wanted as my world would only now allow me a glimpse of my Beloved. This is a time where a mask is held with heavy smolder of confusion over our minds. I understood him only as something different, for he kept me intrigued, though I could not understand the context of this (only that I was absorbed with his presence).

It was the feeling of always wanting more of him when I was in his presence and I could never get enough of him at the same time. For this meeting of our love coming together solidified and cemented our essence of who we were as one, but as one, the stronghold of insecurities of love could not withstand without the defeat of understanding what the substance of this love was inherently showing us. We were one form of another, the other of each other. What did this mean, as we had not a clue? For love, what is love in the eyes of the beholder? Is it only a feeling, or is it something more, a memory perhaps, a metaphor of this so-called lineage of time?

I might have asked myself so early on in this romance, for to the world, love was that of the simple mind, the type of love one understands as exponential. But to understand this love would be to understand us, for I had no idea of the wicked nature of the context of love. For love had not found me until now and us, who was "us"? This would be the key to the understanding of our story. If love were what I had believed love to be, I would have quickly been taught the many lessons of real love and its very powerful conquest. For that conquest of love would have become the realities of my life's purpose and mission after this initial phase of meeting.

As with anything that is true, the natural form of the elements of love…it is difficult to fathom this love for the connection of it had a mystical nature; it was something about London's eyes that would set in motion the literal connotation of the effects of this love. The meaning of something that was far beyond my mind's abilities to ascertain, as this was the beginning of the expansion of subliminal messages that would be shared with me in words of affirmative nature with figurative denotation.

19

Scene I

The day would change the totality of my existence as I knew it. It was late in the evening. My mind could not stop thinking about the policeman, London, that I had met earlier in the day. Never would I look back on this day and not understand the impact on my life this one single day would have, and just as the day is promised, so is the night. This would be the theme that we would traverse on this journey of the fool, for a leap of faith would be the very thing that would conquer us, and it would also be the very thing that would guide us in synergy. What was this kinship to a person? I would beg the answer from myself.

For it purely was the nature of his wit that found a connection to the oscillation of sound in me. There was a sense of sweet muse to his voice, and yet something more. It was this extraordinary element of pleasure to his kindred spirit. For it was the counsel of wit that would stir my fondness, and it was something more, an illusion of fate, perhaps?

A noble name...London (even his given name found a harmony with me). His name sent a message to my heart, a fleeting lullaby, a mingling of his melody...the very first night I met him. It was to be in touch with this sense of stimuli as he gave this feeling of recognition. It was what awoke my senses to him, as I found sentiment in his words, even in the very first message he sent me.

Further I ponder the thought of him, for it was his ability with words and self-expression that caught my attention. But it was also something more, for our words were not just words, as the context was from somewhere beyond. The words we shared would become that of a complex wisdom and these words would change both of our lives forever as the keenness or desire of our soul would be the acme of our intelligence.

In the time of our union, our conversations would be that of understanding us and would surpass that of which we knew and what we knew to be. To be was what would need to be relevant to our knowing of what was, as "what was" would be revealed, in the ability to recognize "what is" which meant to accept what it is "to be." Naturally, our style of communication would begin effortlessly and pleasantly. The element of a wholesome allure…mental stimulation, for the insight of our knowing would need to expand into our mind of memory. Our planes of our coming together is what would stimulate the expanse of such mere mindfulness, as our minds expanded to the wonders of this love. For this was the expression of our inherent desire of each other, as that, in fact, was the alchemy to this union. Who we were to each other would be something far more profound, as it was the transcendence of all understanding. For what this union represented surpassed our minds' understanding, as it would be to understand spirituality and to give a premonition. This love was not a love of anything we knew, so our awareness would need to expand from its constrained mindset of 3-D.

London's character was like a song of muse, what to make of him, I wasn't sure…nor did he of me. My eyes took in his presence and my mind took in his character. He was witty, I noticed that right away. His disposition was pleasant and sophisticated. He felt comfortable to be around and he was easy to talk to. His words and personality are articulate and charming. As London would be one of the strongest of characters I would ever encounter, there was the quality of the one thing that stands out the most in him: He speaks his mind without holding anything back. I'm not quite sure how to take this from such a strong-minded soul as this would play a role in the perplexing mystical element of the union. To understand this element would be to understand one of the layers of our time. Yet, I found this to be a virtue in him, to say whatever was on his mind without discretion, and I understand this was a special quality. It was his confidence; he believed in himself on a very fundamental level and I admired that about him. I could define him by a single word. Inherently, he is *indifferent*. This word was his personified character, his personality, the way he carried himself in his exchange in communication and furthermore, it was his state of mind.

I wanted to get to know London better, so I invited him to come for a walk with me the next morning on the Virginia Corridor Trail where we first laid eyes on one another. As our story is that of figurative nature and obscure understanding, this would be where we meet again as the translation of this meeting point found us in a different reality and with a different awareness of understanding us.

He agreed and we met outside of my house. As we walked, I noticed he was looking me over, but mainly what I noticed is who he is and how comfortable this first meeting was and that we mindlessly became submerged in conversation. We are like old friends. Our dialogue goes from talking about us a little to talking about the future, to talking about relationships. I was dying for a coffee and asked London if he wanted to grab a coffee. He agreed and we were on our way. He allowed me to order first and as I put in my order, he looked at me, surprised. He said, "That's funny. That's my order." He looked over at the barista and said, "I'll have the same thing." I smiled at him and I was thinking it quite odd that we like the same drink, White Chocolate Mocha…go figure.

We grabbed our drinks and continued our walk. We reached a part of the trail where there were some big redwood trees. I asked him if he would like to take a break and sit down to drink our coffees. It was the perfect setting. We relaxed and I noticed him putting one of his arms back and he leaned into it and took in the scenery. I watched him and took him in. He took a deep breath, and he looked very peaceful, but as I was looking at him, I noticed something. I wanted to know why he felt so familiar to me. I was looking at his face for a reason and I didn't see one. I came back to my thoughts and I was wondering if it was something else. I think maybe there was something about him that I found attractive, so I searched his face again, but that was not it either.

He looked at me and said, "Tell me something about yourself."

I said, "Well, ask me something that you would like to know."

He said, "Okay…what are you looking for in a person?"

I look at him for a little bit of clarity because that is a loaded question, but I saw that he wasn't going to give any and this question was for me to answer with what my mind gave me. He wanted to know exactly that. That was, in fact, the bigger question behind the question… where was my state of mind? My answer was about as loaded as the question. I gave him a long-winded answer. I said, "Well, I want a partner, someone I can count on, someone with the same outlook on life as me, someone that I could build something with, and who I can fall in love with and be in love with, someone with the same goals, same values, same drive, and who has similar likes as me." I also added, "Someone who likes and enjoys the same hobbies I have, like traveling, and likes to do the same things I like to do, like working out." I go on to say: "I'm not shallow and I don't look for someone who is physically attractive. What attracts me most about a man is his mind."

I turned around and asked him the same question and he replied, "Well, all of the things you just said, but with different names." I asked him to explain, and he said, "Well, you say 'partner' and I say, 'best friend,' but the one thing that is most important in all of the things you just said is the company."

I looked to him to offer me greater understanding, and he said, "Well, yeah, for example, when you travel and do all of these things you like to do, it's all about the company. If you are with the wrong company, they will make it miserable, but if you are with the right company, they will make it meaningful. You see, it's all about the company!"

His wisdom astonished me. I thought about this for a moment and I understood the bigger picture behind his words. He's a deep thinker and I was instantly attracted to his mind. As I write this part of my story, I am taken back by his wisdom and the beauty of his mind. That was actually and truly the inspiration behind this book. The spot we are sitting at where we had our first heart-to-heart would be one of my favorite places to come and visit and remember him by, in times of separation. I would come here to find solace, to find him in memory, to find serenity for my mind and peace for my heart.

The Illusion of Our Time

To be in the presence of him, my London, it is the harmonics of the heavens, the spheres of the celestial sounds of harmony of our soul notes coming together like that of the Fibonacci Sequence: the golden spirals of consciousness. Being in his presence was to uncover the idea of the energetic matrix that made us. To understand would be to start at the beginning…at the meeting point of zero. This was the awareness to convey the space of the cosmos, for it was in this realm where the sounds of his presence in me turned to the radiance of love…the sacred dance we do with each other would be the equilibrium we reach in energetic harmony, for this is something we can feel on a deep level of intuitive nature, separate from the physical. This was the breath of life in us, our vitality in one another. It was the coming together of the Xs and numbers, mathematic formulations to create the whole of the experience of the nature of love, awakening the evolutionary process of the 1111, the sacred gate to the code of us.

We meet again as we set this stage of this romance, a new foundation, as we have made the connection and now, we are like friends from a long time ago; this story is that of his kindred spirit in me. To distinguish this was also to recognize spiritual science, as our intellect of science begins to do this dance of a mystical nature with comprehension of spirit, with connection to mind. There is an association being made: It is to the intelligence of the mind, but the mind is not open to such conception, though this dance of the minds cultivates and the energy that is exchanged ferments in the realm of creative nature an awareness of a new sort of energy, the connection of spirit and science.

This energy was the key and the force that would drive this dance of entangled desires of the mind, heart, and soul. This was unbeknownst to us at the time, for the mask of desire has its face only of that, standing with incredible allure. We came to a meeting place of point zero. Here the exchange of that conversation takes place, but the real exchange is something else, for our mask only allows us to surface-touch this idea, as we are trying to figure out what it is that feels out of sorts, for we are existing in this new space of being together, this space of uniting with our one true love.

One gleaming aspect of him was how easy it felt—and feels—to be around him. It was something about him, the quality of everything about him, all at once. We felt the pull, a natural magnetic type of pull that we have for and with each other. One may describe this as a way to understand how attractions of nature work, the positive and negative energies, the female and masculine polarities. It is to understand polarity consciousness where everything is seen in twos: love and hate, good and evil, religion and science, wake and sleep. For with the drive of one of these, the perfect match of the other in its respective place is like finding the magic key to love, lived only to tell in the sexual expression of a manifested energy of surge. It is a natural love attraction, the laws of nature. We found it is the element of refinement...the rawness of natural elements (fire, earth, water, and air).

These elements rendered the feeling that took me to a portal of a new life, as the byproduct of these elements render the principles of metal in combination to each other, that of hot and cold and dry and moist. For this life is in perfect synchronization, the 1111 of us, as this is with true love's purpose. To be in this energy is to bring us together, but the fine balance left to the tugs of push and pull and the natural elements that were the byproduct would dictate the forces of nature between us.

To be in front of him and to hear him talk, I was submerged in his mind of wonder as he spoke with articulate purpose. The tone of his words was that of the pulsation of pleasure in my spirit. We had just met, but it was as if I knew him from the past. I just stared at him and read him like a book, as he would become my book of poetic nature of the soul, for he synchronized in me all the elements of the refinement of the palate…the arrangement of words of splendid vibrancy of a cosmic cast.

What was it to be in his presence of poetic nature? It was to take in the words of meaning of the inborn quality of seeded nature. For it was a time to implant these seeds as harvest would be the time to reap the signature of what has been cultivated in fruitage.

Knowledge was the seeded nature of this union and with each of our meetings it would be for this, that our creative ability would become the acquisition of the sowing into each other, but with that came effort. What kind of meaning was my mind opening to as awareness is stripped from our minds and the meaning itself is exposed down to only a fathom of idea that existed in the intellect of our design? The effort, a reward of the ability to open the mind to what was, the "what was" would be to understand what it was that we were seeing in front of us, how to see through the dawning of mask, for it was not through sight alone that we would comprehend this bond.

Who was this man? He felt way too familiar, for that would be the significance of him; embedded in my thoughts somewhere was a nostalgic air. He felt too comfortable, too distinctive. What was his association to me? This is what my mind was opening to understand as our paths had not crossed by casual means. Nor were his words of a casual nature, for when he spoke, each of his words would hit a note of chord in my soul that would vibrate and send a message of the inherent draw of something reminisced. He had a way with words and a way with his sensible ability to conceptualize, as he, too, would stare back at me in a gaze of equivalent muddle, as he also is prying his mind of intellect, but our masks were placed firmly over us, blurring what was standing there. We became acquainted to this spiritual space. It was the spiritual space of time we were embarking upon, to bring forth a new concept of illusion of us, the science of God awakening in us.

Scene II

One of the most wonderful experiences of my life was the short time I was able to spend with London, slowly getting to know him and who he was. It was a fascinating time. He kept me intrigued; I always wanted more of him and this connection.

Our connection was (and remains) strong. It was imbued with a sense of a knowing, but from a long time ago. One could not conjure the illusion of what this meant, for it was the moment of keen arousal to something familiar. A sense of wedlock, if you will, to the unraveling of mystery. It would be to start in the entanglement of the vision and foresight of the eye to unlocking the magic of the gates of reason.

We wanted to see each other again and his becoming over me was a fond, gentle stir of emotions that caught the sight of noble intrigue over my wonder, as it was his personality and charming ways that sent this air of muse. It would be in the succession of thought, the rite to my knowing of the spirit of toil, for it would be to understand many layers to find and uncover who he was to my heart, as his sweet ripple of residence would find a theme of the force of love within me.

One observation I made about London was that he seemed to be on no timeline. There was this sense of no haste for anything. It felt very relaxing and laid-back being around him. We both wanted to see the other again, and I was beginning to like many things about him. So, we conversed over the phone and decided to go out for a bit. He asked me to pick a place, so I decided on a fun restaurant that was nearby called B.J.'s. He asked if he should pick me up or if I wanted to meet him there. I thought about it for a minute and said, "If I'm going to have a cocktail, you better pick me up." He understood and said, "No problem. I'll text you when I'm on my way."

He showed up in a Chevy Tahoe Suburban and we drove toward our destination. We were having an easy conversation, and he told me what he likes to do for fun. He has a passion for guns, and he couldn't talk about this subject enough. He started to tell me about a gun show that he attends with a friend every year. He gave me insight into the preparation and what goes into these types of shows. I listened to him, but obviously, I had very little to say because I had no knowledge about guns, but I saw the enthusiasm he has for what he does, and I admired this about him.

We arrived at B.J's, a local restaurant and bar, and ordered drinks. I found that we had another similarity as we began to drink and converse. The conversation was easy and comfortable and one thing I could tell about London was that he possessed a unique characteristic: he was unconventional and it was a quality that was mirrored in me. The more we drank, the more he got to know the other side of me. I'm very fun when I drink, and I could see how much he was picking up on this. He was really taking in the change in my attitude and in my verbal exchanges. I could see the way he reacted to this in his expressions, and I don't think he expected it from me. I can handle my alcohol well, but I'm also quite entertaining and lively. I laugh a lot, and I just let loose. I say incredibly random things and he liked this and thought it was funny. We laughed about it all. The mood was light and unexpected, and I think that's what made it so enjoyable. Clearly, we had an awesome first date. When it was time to go, he took me home and we experienced a very entertaining episode of tipsy me.

The seats in his truck are very high and my dress was short and tight. I was trying to be ladylike and graceful, but I was too tipsy to know the difference. I was wondering how I was going to get out of his truck without flashing him or falling out altogether. So I moved closer to the side and swung my legs around, but my dress rolled up. I tried to pull it down, but it wouldn't go down. I needed to get out so I didn't fall out, but I was completely flashing him. I reacted and just jumped out of the truck. I was still struggling with my dress because it was rolled up and as I was trying to figure this out, I dropped my purse. I had a big black purse that I carried around with me everywhere and it was heavy and had my life in it.

My bag fell to the floor, and I didn't know what to do. My dress was all tangled and I was flashing him. My purse was on the ground and

I knew I needed to pick It up. I realized I must look stupid right now, so what was I to do? I knew that if I bent over to pick up my purse, my dress was just going to roll up higher. I looked up at him because I honestly didn't know what to do, and London was giving me the most hysterical look I've ever seen. It was like "Chick, are you for real?" I could see him scratching his head like, "Lord, help this girl." I wanted to laugh, but I didn't know at whom. Maybe at myself, maybe at the scene, maybe at his reaction, as the whole thing was completely comical.

I realized it didn't even matter anymore what I did because all I knew is this was painful for him to watch and he was dying for me to figure this out so he could just leave, but he needed me to make it to my door first. I needed to put him out of his misery, so I bent over and picked up my purse and allowed my dress to roll up because it didn't matter. We didn't exchange words. He simply waited for me to walk to my door and let myself in. I saw him drive off, but that look he had on his face during this encounter would be the look I recognize him by. It would be the look my mind would register in its memory bank as London's "crazy cop look." This look would become very familiar to me and it would be one that I got very acquainted with as time passed.

The symbolism of the day would elude me at the time, but in looking back, my black bag was my baggage: all my dark secrets, regrets, and disappointment of which I couldn't let go. In an instant, they fell to the ground, my whole life. And London was there to help me figure it out and deal with all those things that I carried with me in my big black bag of life. I had to choose to pick it up again. I had to choose what to do with eyes on me just like London's eyes were on me at that moment. I had to make a choice, and I had to walk away with that choice. I couldn't continue to live and do the things I had done in my life up to that point. I would have to make changes, big changes, and I would have to lighten my load. My purse was heavy. I didn't need half of the stuff I carried around with me; in fact, I didn't need any of it. I needed to lighten the load and huge changes were in store for me.

This process of change was going to take a while. Part of this process would be fun and a bit comical at times, but most of it would be painful and confusing. Most importantly, though, was that I had London, and he was not going to allow me to go through this alone. He would be there for me until I figured this out on my own; that was his message to me. He was going to watch, and he was going to make sure I made it to my door. As painful as it may have been to watch at times, he was not going to leave me until he knew I would be okay.

Our first date was the beginning of our time together in the physical realm. It felt like each day after brought forth lifetimes of memories which continued to shed light to the allure of who we were to each other.

Remembering My Beloved, A Memory of a Distant Past: The Energy of Eve

London and I felt our connection on a deep level. It was a pull for one another, but it was also something more. From the start, this connection began to test our morals, ethics, and principles while an ordeal of conformity was fermenting. We would need to break free from its grip to open our minds to natural instinct without the arbitrary judgment from our culture and our civilization at this present time. The truth was that London's character was of a defiant nature, which shed light on the qualities of the Divine Masculine; those qualities equal the natural laws of him as he made himself known to me. All the while, the experience provoked the mind principle of the "now" time of us, for London's presence would leave an impression that would ensue…the now of us, as all things co-exist by way of eternity, a time with no end.

However, reality is that of the now and "now" is our life and time in me—and him in me—and together through us: the concept of our evolutionary path of the here and now. Like time, a moment lived and a memory of the past; so is the future a time to live, but in the now of meaning as I lifted his name in the evolution of us. But first, we must break away from the linear conception of thought and awaken the concept of activation as the linear interchanges with the cyclic interval. As time was not elusive, it was with purpose and meaning. It was the messages to be heard and the memories and emotions to be captured as that of a moment of time.

London was also everything of a defiant nature and so I didn't know what to make of him, only that he was always on my mind. At this point, this stillness in thought is that of the "I am" concept, as this is the new shadow of reflection in likeness. He was not only on my mind, as my body is a reflection of my mind's appearance and so my body's energy gravitates to this man. But I remember one thing above all, his sensual touch, for he finds in me a place of emotion that awakens my memory to this energy of Eve. My eyes were opened to divine knowledge of procreation, the forbidden fruit of our sexuality.

We started to spend a lot of time together. My body felt an allure of passion for him, but I didn't know what to make of this. This secret, this intense sexual force, that brought us together divides itself and creates needs and waves of powerful desire. I feel this man now, both in his elusive nature and in his presence, as this was the paradoxical influence that lived over us from now onto this day forward: He was my Adam. It was the natural way of getting to know someone slowly, spending time in the other's presence, talking to each other, talking about ourselves and letting our minds be an open book about our pasts and the different experiences that made us who we were.

With this communication, it would open my mind up to the Trinity: The three expressed as one and the alchemy being the sexual force that arose in us and the animal desires of the other, as the Kundalini also rose and began awakening this new energy and way of life. As we entered the new energies of sacred places, the energy and nature of this relationship was sparked, and with the delicious bliss would also come the unbearable pain. Powerful desires would open our eyes to shame and the knowledge of true suffering and the total void. The serpent of sexual fire would both create and destroy while we mustered the willpower to bear it while drinking the wine of ferment of enlightenment, divine order, and divine will.

I had a significant observation at this time. It felt as if we already knew each other, but we were only confirming what we already knew. That reflected on how fast this process of getting to know one another occurred. The connection that had pulled us together became cemented now in this journey of learning what we already knew. Our planes had connected, but these planes had a memory that was familiar…it just had to remember. This pull, however, was difficult to decipher because it was hard to understand this different plane, as our minds were newly rediscovering it, and the other. It came across to us as wanting to be in a relationship with this person, but at the same time, it felt like I had already been married to this man. Confusing and conflicting messages began to manifest in my mind, and they were expressed through mixed feelings that materialized on the surface.

Scene III

London and I developed a fast friendship and we had been dating a while. I was starting to like a lot of things about him. We messaged each other often and met up for lunch and coffee breaks, but tonight he invited me to his home for a quiet evening of alone time. London was so familiar to me; the feeling was that of having been with him sometime in the distant past, but the only way I could describe it in my awareness of this present time was that I felt as if I already knew him, but it was only confirming what I already knew each time we would meet. This reflected to us in the process of getting to know one another. It felt like a connection that had pulled us together, only we had very little control over the deep emotions that would emerge from the union.

When I arrived, he cordially invited me in, and we sat in his living room. On the walls there were picture frames with family portraits. We started the evening off by talking about the pictures on the walls. This escaped me at the time, but London was letting me in to his lifetime of memories. I could see that he hailed from a long family history of the military, and he himself was a former soldier. I could see these qualities and characteristics clearly exhibiting in him; he is a warrior by nature. He had a sword on his wall, and he talked to me about how he collects swords as a hobby. He also has a life-size statue of a soldier in his living room, holding a shield and a smaller sword. London told me he had recently remodeled his living room, theming it after his life. I saw him for what he was and is: a fighter, a trooper, and in a sense, a rebel. I began to understand his character more. Of course, it all made sense: ex-military, police officer, and a gun enthusiast.

He asked me to sit on the couch with him as he turned on the TV. He said, "Do you care to watch a movie, or should we watch something on TV?" I replied, "I'm okay with whatever you'd like to do." He offered a few movie choices and we decided on "Troy." I like this type of movie and I could see this flick would be the closest to anything we would mutually like. We started the movie, but we ended up talking instead. As we got more comfortable, I realized that I was tired, and I asked if we could go lie down on his bed.

The Door to Eden

This pervasive love and attraction to what I now know is the other half of my soul—which is embodied in London—is perplexing. It was and is somewhat elusive, and it felt skewed somehow. The familiarity of it suggested that the connection was always written in the stars. The pull and the affinity toward each other meant that we would experience a different kind of attraction: It was like a magnet and the pull was an energy force, like pure life-force energy. It was the most natural bond, a bond of instant connection, and it came with a supernatural energy and intensity like nothing I'd ever known or experienced before, only that it had a mystical nature and I felt it on an etheric level. It was like coming face-to-face with one's own self, only the polar opposite. It was always that feeling of comfort, a feeling like you had already known this person in a different way, in a different place, in a different time; it was a feeling of nothing but absolute acceptance, for better or for worse. It was a burning desire, a connection of deep love, trust, devotion, and the ease of being in his presence.

At this early stage, things felt very misunderstood; however, though we had a strong enticement to the other, there was something that didn't quite conceptualize. This left us feeling intrigued, and we wanted more of the other. It was like being in tune with him, but not understanding the connection. This was true of the relationship, where nothing made sense because it defied words and logic as we got more involved. Confusion set in amidst all the pleasure.

It was the concept of the conscious polarity that arose, the one of two. It was the role of fate and of holy nature that was being shown to us, the separation of two, the male and female polarity, the energetic

35

individual in each other, the push-pull and pull-back. The pull was like a magnetic field of energy, fed by the sexual energy that was awakening within us. There was something very mysterious about the bond. We both felt this, but we couldn't put our finger on what it was, so we continued to try to figure it out. It was the lure of the force of sexual attraction, the act of nature's purest form of virtuosity, for the mystery of it would also be one of the clues to the door of Eden, to the door of our truth.

Both truths would play a pivotal role. In the Great Arcanum, which represented the mystery of the physical and spiritual worlds, this great secret is seen in the mirror of us, but it was fiercely protected by a veil that was held firmly over our eyes. This knowledge would be that of sexual magic. The knowing of who we were together would allow us to traverse the brutal instinct of the sexual body into passionate emotions of astral love, as our minds were left to feel this in the primal nature of the wild animal within.

The serpent of truth wrapped tightly around us, coming up from the soil, from the ground below. This serpent knowledge would be the gatekeeper of the mystical nature of great works as the deep-seated secret, that of life-force energy, as it was left to ponder in the balance. In this balance we would find out who we were in each other and how we related to the other, and further, with the higher levels of understanding, how we related to this love, through our minds, as the serpent continued its awakening of the conscious, awakened mind. As with allegorical meaning, we were ready to set this in motion with a new understanding of who we are. For now, this astuteness is what stood in the way of the life-works and the rarity of our relationship.

Within the heart would be the place where this would start; this is where the spark of creation would commence, and where the groundwork would begin. The white owl of sacred wisdom would fly up from the underground world, as both good and bad exist in this world and the heart would be the place to understand this energy of duality...the conscious mind where the transmutation of the energy of creation would take place. This foundation of deep-rooted

soil would give way to the priestess of self-init′
of change, the water of the alchemist woul′
emotion of change would be amplified with ene₁ᵤ
of psychic abilities of intuitive nature, the scroll ot ᵥ
bring about the two pillars of strength to stabilize the heart ᵥ
the polarity of creation. Through the heart would be the abᵤ
embrace and see the mysteries of wisdom that exist in the union ᵤ
opposites, the good and the bad, the yin and yang, the all of creation,
the all of that in balance, and following out of that, the liberation
of spirit when in unity. Like the full circle of all things, we rotate
as the fluids solidify, creating the balance of nature's perfect sphere
and all things in it, the sustainer of all things created. To the mind,
nature acts as the messenger, for it renders from these things both
the visible and invisible; all join, manifold, in the witness of love.
Both the heavens and the earth join in and with them, the truths and
domains of esoteric nature.

We would start our connection in the 3-D, but the 5-D would be
where the stabilization of these energies took place, in the higher
vibrational realms. All the time spent in the journey of healing would
be in preparation with shifting our energy and allowing of thoughts
and feelings to evolve and sustain in these higher frequencies. This
purpose would connect us to the powers of the divine, where we
could exist fluidly in each other.

In turn, this healing would lead us back to new beginnings, for the
foundation of this love is rooted deep inside and transmuted in the
solidification of love, and that of the purest of elements. As with this
new autonomy overcoming our minds, so too came the understanding
of the different dimensions or the different states of consciousness,
a new grid of foundational thought, a new intelligence rendered
to us through the union of us. However, we would need to wrap
our minds around this intelligence and the vibrational frequencies
that we would reach, as it all became part of a new reality in us and
through us. It would be on the different dimensions of frequency
that we would understand our love. For to get this right would be
our work of that of the other. The third dimensional aspect would be

loop of time, where in it would strengthen our love, but what was rt in the balance would need to also get to the stage of the elixir of immortality, a universal solvent of the soul.

To get to our balance as twins, we would need to reach the 5-D, where unconditional love exists, and we could experience this through each other. It would be necessary to reconnect with classic antiquity, nature, and ancient wisdom to understand what would happen next in this union. Through theurgy,* which is the practice of rituals to connect to the divine and our higher deities to bring understanding of the supernatural, the divine, and sacred nature, an understanding of our God and Goddess powers that exist within.

As such, we would enter an ancient age of the celestial calendars of time...a walk-through of time. Here is where our love existed, in that cosmic time and in the celestial bodies of time: the sun, moon, planets, and stars also offer the passage of time throughout our existence. It is here, where our time is cyclical and full circle is the understanding of who we are to the other. It would be our ancient wisdom of understanding our evolution, as the motion of these energetic bodies brought forces that would also determine the seasons and ages of our discovery of the unfolding of many secrets of virtue. We align in this time, in the celestial system of the cosmic heart, as it is our season, and this is our constellation. Cosmic energies line up for the awakening of our energetic system, as London, too, would be the constellation of all things concentric, with that of the heartspace of our celestial sphere. With the heart being that which holds the greatest of electricity, the passage to alignment had come to pass.

---

* *Theurgy describes the practice of rituals, sometimes seen as magical in nature, performed with the intention of invoking the action or evoking the presence of one or more deities, especially with the goal of achieving henosis (uniting with the divine) and perfecting oneself.*

Scene IV

"Do you want to go lay down on the bed?" London repeated this back, as if he was thinking out loud. I could see his face change as he took this in, and then his "cop expression" came over his face. He looked unsure almost immediately after he said it, and then he verbalized this expression. He said, "Are you sure?"

I replied, "Yeah, why not? I'm really tired. I've had a long day and I'd love to lay down."

He smiled and said, "Okay, if that's what you want."

He showed me around his room now, and he told me how his bedroom is set up the way the rooms are set up at his favorite hotel where he stays when he goes to gun shows every year. I think it's cool that he's creative in this way. He designed his room in a modern, fun, and high-tech way that resembles an upscale hotel. The closet is off to the side and I can see how organized he is. Everything was in its place. I could see his military side at work as there was nothing that didn't have a spot. But it felt very much like a man's room, a man who knows exactly what he likes.

He sat on his bed and said he'd like to show me what he likes to watch on TV. He said, "Sit and relax." He found a show, a series about Medieval times. I was curious about it; it's like the movie "Troy" that we had just been watching. He said, "Let's watch the latest episode and I'll catch you up."

I liked this idea. I wanted to hear London tell me a story. I wanted to hear his take and get into his mind a little. I am more interested in hearing London tell his version of this show than I was interested in the actual show. I listened to him describe how the soldiers were fighting this battle over a kingdom, but in retrospect, the battle is over the girl who has been promised to one of the kings. But as always, love is not easy, and the girl was in love with one of the kings from the other side and now the battle is really over the girl. I looked at him, smiled, and said, "Isn't that the way life is? The real battle is always about our heart."

London leaned over and kissed me. I closed my eyes and kissed him back. I never realized how attracted I was to him until he kissed me. Our lips came together, and he opened my mouth with his kiss. He melted into my mouth with his tongue. My eyes started to bat, and I had to open them again because his kiss was amazing. I loved the way he kissed me. It was seductive and it was done in a very purposeful manner, like he knew exactly the way I would want him to kiss me. He didn't have to figure it out; he already knew. The way his tongue moved in my mouth was exquisite. It was like a mint chocolate, sweet with a hint of freshness. I closed my eyes and it felt like we were having a meeting of the mind as we were kissing, like he was reading my thoughts.

My mind was present in this moment and I told myself that this felt like déjà vu, like we were old lovers who had lost each other and were now found. With this kiss came an overflowing passion, and it made me long for him. But I wondered why I was feeling this way from just his kiss.

As the kisses became more passionate and intense by the second, the mood shifted a little as I looked into his eyes. I saw so much lust in his eyes, but then I saw something else and the intensity scared me a little. I saw a look in his eyes, something I had never seen before, and I wasn't sure what to make of it. I closed my eyes in order to not get distracted and I was feeling this moment. He started to get more comfortable with me, touching me very sensually. First, he went very slowly and then he began touching me everywhere. I opened my eyes again, and I saw that look; though it was difficult to discern, it looked a little like madness. But what I felt was passion and this was the message being conveyed by his body to mine. He was overcome with it, with pure pleasure. He bit down on his lower lip and stared at me. I saw that he liked it when I had my eyes open. He looked at my reactions and I could see very much that he was studying me and letting his instincts direct this subtle dance between us.

Our Telepathic Connection is Born

London and I find ecstasy in coming together; it is like we are of the caduceus,* or the "staff of Hermes," as we wind around each other in mesmerizing energy. This coming together is like being taken back in time. We are imbued with a feeling of nostalgia, a feeling of ancient existence, and as the snakes interlace, it awakens something in us. It means we would understand the metaphysical nature of us as one. The symbol represents healing, and he made me feel whole; he made me feel complete. I feel him as he births a universal sphere around us, one of sacred nature. It is a union of duality coming together at the top, as our minds feel the energy that pulls us together. As one, we embody this sacred representation of the antenna of truth and love.

This feeling releases within us, as our water signs solidify and the emotional body comes over us, yielding insight into who we truly are, as we awaken from within. I have the distinctive feeling of remembering as our senses become even more sensitive and I remember smelling dirt: the scent of reverting and coming back down to the soil, the snakes' natural habitat. We understand that the seeds buried within this soil contain fertile wisdom and knowledge. It is the Lemurian seed crystals that store the knowledge of our discovery of each other, but to understand this would be to understand how to communicate with the crystal energy messages and how to decode this story of our time. It would be through the gridding of crystals that we would create a natural vortex, a different way of communicating, and this was now being shown to us.

---

*   *Caduceus: An ancient Greek or Roman herald's wand, typically one with two serpents intertwined around it, carried by the messenger god Hermes or Mercury.*

This rebirth, the primal nature of communication, that is relinquished through the sphere that came around us is that of our ancient existence, as the process of remembering starts to unfold. It is a remembering of our natural self and our existence of a solidification of time through that of our most innate being. It is a dialogue that we experience in this space that cements this to our minds early on. This lost land is like that of the Lemurian culture. Our souls, in a state of shock, have found the other. It is the sphere of the Pacific Ring of Fire that is born again out of the emotional body as we begin to remember what is beneath the rolling, restless seas. It is in this communication, the mysteries of forgotten sophistication, from a long time ago. All the hidden treasures, the lost remnants of wisdom, are being discovered and uplifted in spirit as the legend of an ancient civilization falls over our reminiscence.

This grid of visualization creates our realities and the concurrent experience of these worlds of all of time find us and bring with it a feeling of déjà vu. Our souls come together as one to join and cross these grids to give our existence a new meaning, like a rising out of the sea of creation, the flow of collective consciousness. All the years of collective, submerged knowledge finds us now, the mystery of oceanic erosion, as the sea walls vanish and let us in. The energy is that of mystery, illusion, the enchantment of the underwater, and the nature of water.

The energy, like that of water, the inherent substance, is everything liquid and change is the flow of its nature. It is experienced like a sea of chaotic elements. The emotions take hold of us and the counterbalance of each is a random and undecided battle of both. We are solidified as one to find the fate of the tide, to turn to the emotional balance of love. Love would be the way to balance these energies in a calm, evolved, and succeeding tide, carrying the message in a bottle that finally reaches its intended heir. What would take place next was water enchantment, and to us in union, it was a spiritual representation of change in us as one.

It would be through this communication of messages that we come to a standstill within our souls to truly see and hear the message being granted to us, in this deep sea of mystery, the deep sea of secret wisdom. Our connection to all of it comes from each other, the other of the compound, the sphere of currents.

We now find this space in the other. This is the first time I experienced this new language with my Beloved. It is my initial account of it, but we wouldn't understand the level, the power, of internal connection. It is the water flow, the liquification, that begins to flow and shifts us into a liquid form of spiritual energy that starts from within us. It is the intuitive power of water divination that changes our minds and transforms our way of thinking. However, this knowledge is released to us in the way of divine timing when we would understand our relationship better.

Scene V

He took my shirt, bunched it up in his hands, pulled it over my head, peeling it off my arms in a very assertive way. He put his arm behind my back and lay me down on his pillow and continued to kiss me, but his hands were under my bra. His touch was both rough and erotic at the same time; he was in the process of discovering me while completely taking in the moment. He was very present and alive. Grabbing me a bit forcefully, he pulled me to the edge of his bed. He brought his hands up to my arms and lifted them over my head. As he was doing so, he held me down with one of his arms, completely taking control. He pulled my skirt up and I could feel his hands on my underwear. I felt him pull my panties to the side and we lost ourselves in that moment. I didn't expect this, so it took me a second to regain my bearings. I was thinking, "What is this?" The shared passion was wild, crazy, and untamed.

I felt like London was arresting me, and at the same time, I was being seduced. Actually, I was confused. While my mind contemplated my lack of clarity, he pleasured my body. He reached up and put his hand around my throat. I was a bit shocked and my eyes got big. I looked at his face and I saw those crazy eyes again. In his eyes, I could see pure lust. I felt his hand put some pressure on my neck. I was feeling a bit violated but aroused at the same time. I looked to his face, but I could see that crazy look again and I had to turn my eyes away. Yet, and still, the feelings emanating were the most sensual feeling I've ever felt. The combination of this force, pleasure, and violation—all at the same time—was condescending madness, yet it was packaged as the most tactile, most seductive, most unbelievable sexual pleasure and experience of my life. London was focused on reading me and then pleasuring me. His eyes began to get wider and wider as he saw in my face that I was utterly lost in this moment with him. Then, and only then, he allowed himself to release.

When we were done, we were both breathing heavy. My eyes rolled back as if to make the statement, "That was unbelievable." We looked at one another and recognized that this connection was something different, like nothing we'd ever known or experienced before. We understood it only at the time as a strong sexual attraction to the other, but the intensity was beyond explanation and understanding.

This moment awakened in me the dual nature that we shared, for it was through the magical experience of him and his sexuality that awakened the sleeping DNA of us. This woke us to the Adam and Eve connection, the portal of the 1111, and the energy produced from this union was that of a sacred nature. While the energy was being fully developed, I was born again with divine fire, as the connection illuminated within me and transmuted to that of pure energy. "Just breathe," I told myself as I stared back at his eyes in disbelief. The sexual energy felt like pure life-force, like pure vitality.

As I was reflecting on this moment, London said the most compelling comment. He looked me in the eyes, picking himself up and said, "Ah...you're a people pleaser."

I sat up and said, "Excuse me?" He started to get dressed, and so did I. He turned to face me, and he said, "Yeah, that was the most selfless sex I've ever had." My eyes got big because I didn't know what to make of his words. I had no words. I was dumbfounded.

I wanted to say something to him because I was so insulted by his blunt observation, but I wasn't sure what to say. I had no words for his words.

Again, though it was early in the relationship, London knew me so thoroughly, but I wouldn't come to that realization until much later.

Nothing Else Mattered

As London and I unite, we enter a new energy field; it is an understanding that no one nor anything else mattered when we are together, because we would become lost in a mystical feeling of love. It was like a circle we would enter, a bubble, where the energies that were unknown to us surge, and only the residual feeling is left behind.

The feeling is our light body being awakened from within, an understanding of the sacred nature of this love. This feeling means to experience everlasting love. It is truth, the rawness of emotion felt not only by the natural impulses of sexual pleasure, but it also opens the heart chakra, and this is felt like a burning sensation that comes from the middle of my chest.

Here is where I meet my Twin: In the divine nature of the beauty of Twin Flame love. This love, this feeling between Twin Flames, happens in the etheric body. It is the merging of the higher self and the subtle bodies. This energy merge is felt like a surge of energy; it is overwhelming to the mind, and many times it is difficult to stay in the moment of sexuality with my Twin because of the overpowering nature that the effects have over my body.

If you haven't felt it yet, the first time you experience this energy exchange with your Twin, you feel the genuine union come to light, but the energies are carried over from a different place and a different time, and they are very difficult to understand and conceptualize. It feels like ecstasy, a true, out-of-this-world, out-of-body experience. This is the feeling of abundance of the soul; it is to touch heaven as my body registers all the light illuminated from within and releases it outward. The gravitational pulls align and there is no division of the soul and no division of the universe around us, for the light surge merges all of this, and the truth of the vibration of love is experienced.

In this Union, your mind finds the connection to the natural world. It is of light; the flame ignites from within. The connection, when it comes together, is the bluest part of a flame. Your mind leaves your awareness and enters a higher place. It is instantaneous and your body fills with the abundance of the pleasure of love. When we are one, it elicits a feeling of completeness, that nothing else mattered.

It is shown to us in this way, the truth of our soul connection... which we experience as complete ecstasy and bliss. It means also to connect to the blueprint of my soul and to feel London, my Twin, on this level, but to not understand the concept, only the feeling of the most powerful release of euphoria. It is like the God and Goddess energy of eroticism, for the love is the ripest form of sexual energy, of fertility, like suited lovers coming together with the strongest passion of natural desires igniting by emotion and fire. This love feels like and is pure pleasure; it is the kindred blaze of two elements, the yin and yang, the black and white, the heat and passion. There exists no boundaries to this erotic nature. It is the cross of the untamed nature of love, the cross of the animal desires of emotion, and we are utterly lost in the madness of this love.

As this shift within us takes place, aspects of the supernatural element of this love begin to shine through us. It is the fire that ignited from within; it feels alive, but our understanding is that of the 3-D realm.

Scene VI

We saw one another again and it was always quite enchanting to look in London's eyes; his eyes would always keep me in rapt attention.

We met again at a local bar and then walked across the street to my store, as it was after hours. As soon as we walked through the door, I could feel my head spinning. He always had this effect on me. It was as if I could not keep my mind "straight" in his presence, nor could I think with clarity. He noticed the effect he had over me and as he sat on a black stool that was off to one side, he said, "You better sit down for a minute." He motioned with his hand and said, "Come here." I walked over to him and he grabbed me, pulling me toward him. I sat on him, as he directed me with his hands, and I wrapped my legs around him, crisscross. We were balancing on each other, and he was looking at me with intrigue.

As we stared into each other's eyes, I put my arms around his neck, and he grabbed me by the hips. We became like the symbol of the caduceus, the "staff of Hermes," as the intertwining serpents became manifest in the physical as the true meaning of the symbol was revealed to our souls and intellect.

I was mesmerized by him and his eyes and we were caught in a shared gaze. I wondered what was going on in that beautiful mind of his and he came in close to kiss me. I smiled at him as I leaned away. I went in to kiss him, and he pulled away and smiled back at me. I wanted to laugh, but I tried again to kiss him because I wanted to taste his mouth and he made me follow him, but he slowly moved from one side to the other. In this moment, he unveiled himself to me; the truth of what he was doing was a truth of us in divine pairing. It was the snakes coming together in harmony at the top of the stake and remembering the truth of who they are to one another. Following this scenario, there would, surprisingly, follow a period of confusion and unending, overwhelming amounts of pain, but first, we would be able to experience the harmony, the beauty, and the divinity of it all.

I liked his game, but I was wondering why he wouldn't kiss me. This would be the theme to the journey of us, me awaiting my Divine Counterpart, only to find him once more with a kiss, while we played this game of us and refined everything contained within us.

I pulled back, holding him by his neck as he held me by my waist. I closed my eyes and leaned back, and I had to trust that he wouldn't let me fall. Trusting him this much felt good: Really, really good. I put my hands over his, and his hands were over my hips. I allowed myself to fall all the way back. He held on tight and I opened my eyes and saw that he was absorbing me, taking me in with his eyes.

He put his hand around my back and brought me up to him, but he was done with his game and he began to kiss me hard. I closed my eyes when we started to kiss, but then after we had been passionately kissing for a minute, I opened my eyes. To my surprise, he had a sort of "madness" in his eyes, and it registered in my mind that his eyes were sort of "skipping."

This look was the same look I'd seen before when we had been intimate, but this time I understood this look to be his soul's eyes that were piercing through him, like a light beam. As London bit his lower lip, I saw his desire for me, and I felt the same way; desire is how he manifested in my body. He pulled me to him, but this time he kissed me even harder. The feeling was that of comfort and longing. He was very inviting, and the effect left me feeling like I'd never ever been kissed before…no, not once, not ever, and never like this. The feeling was unique, of hot passion, yet it held an undercurrent of tranquility. It was like coming home when you know where home is.

We were in a space of pure bliss, and yet, desire lived there, too. He started to kiss my cheek, then his kisses cascaded down to my neck, and then slowly, ever so slowly, descended to my breast. I felt London's mouth, his tongue and lips dancing over my nipples and I looked down at him, and he was looking up at me.

I couldn't stop looking into his eyes, as he held my breast with one hand and started to lick my breast in the most sensual way.

His tongue grabbed my nipple and wrapped around it. With a forceful fit of passion, he put my whole breast in his mouth, and I couldn't stop looking at him. His eyes did not leave mine either. My mouth was open, and I wanted to close my eyes, but I couldn't stop looking into his beautiful eyes. In truth, I couldn't get enough of what he was doing and seeing what my eyes are experiencing. I became numb in this timeless moment of London and me.

He slowly came back up to my mouth and he took it in his. His tongue searched for, and then found my tongue, encircling around it, tugging on it, and then letting it go. He then pulled away.

He put his finger under my chin and pulled my face up to his. He came close as if to kiss me again, but instead, he spoke. He said the most captivating thing: "Can I stalk you?"

I was taken aback. We were looking deeply into each other's eyes and I had so much desire for him at that moment that I would have agreed to almost anything. But I was frozen by this question because I wasn't sure what I was agreeing to. I asked back, "What do you mean?"

Our eyes were dancing together again, and he queried once again, "Can I stalk you?"

I said, "What do you mean?"

London had this crazy look in his eyes, and I was honestly stumped by the question. I couldn't say yes, and I couldn't say no. So, we went in circles with him asking me the question and me answering the question with yet another question. As I searched his face, I wanted and needed to know what he meant before I answered.

Why would a man ask me this question and why would he want to "stalk" me? I wasn't even sure I had heard him correctly the first time he asked. But it was because I couldn't have known at the time what London was really asking.

Eternal Love

From the first moment I met London, two reasons I couldn't stop thinking about him was his mysticism and his "sparkle," both of which captivated me. His charismatic persona opened the light of desire within me, as London possessed an endless, boundless ability to capture me in my imagination and to keep me in a state of mental bliss. In the mystics of this awareness, the heightened experience of knowing purified the knowing of self. It was renunciation that we fight, for logic challenges this knowing as we experience illumination and a conceived self-realization that we cannot refute.

It is us, together, and while we experience the mystical experience of the other, we open into the realm of a new awareness, an exalted path of thought. It is as if London opened my mind to the experience of Medieval times, and it is my imagination that he intensifies. It means we would move into the romance of poetic expression of the earthly realms that captivates this vivid picture of the ingenuity of love. Finding and connecting to London was to find the lover of the one divine, a captivation of the absolute. It feels like belonging, and it is the sheer experience of the elements of love, but this is clouded by unexplained emotions. Further, it is difficult to comprehend, for it is the paradox of love, this dreamy confusion of thought. To feel this love meant to absorb the Deity quality (that of inaccessible intelligence to the mind) and it means to let go of logic.

The hidden meaning of us is concealed; it was like a gift of love in a box, but with no understanding of the mystical element of the supernatural aspect of love contained within its borders. What gives meaning to this boxed love is the assembly of the box. It is a present of antique class, distinguished by its shape, size, and its decorative elements.

The transformation required by this love consumes us and becomes a longing to love without a plea, as this love overtakes the essences of longing, and in turn, raises us to a different expectation as we become attuned to its language.

This love fills us with a natural want; it is fertile soil that is lain before us, as our perception shifts to a primal intuition of sensual love. It feels like a restlessness of self, a desire of animal nature, a surplus of energy, but with tension and stillness combined. It challenges our minds' picturesque aptitude to understand love. It means to transcend human experience. It is in the moment of London and I that the spirit of love unveils its significance of us and to us. We understand the hidden meaning of all things, as the metaphor implies...the center point of all existence is the center point of love. The evanescent aspect of the romance, captivated in light, is like a mosaic window of light rays seen with the eyes of love...where everything is reminiscent of a stage of life where all things shine, even in darkness. This space is where I always found London in my darkest moments. I stand in this light and in the radiance of the darkness. I can see the true color of light, for all the color of insight means seeing London's presence come to luminescence.

I came to know that love exists by way of him; I feel the pain of this love and I understand that London was always in my heart. To delve into the meaning of this love-in-a-box concept is to explore the heart's structure. In the classical antiquity of time, the humanism of the Renaissance represented a time of rebirth. It was in the scholastics that the inference of the human figure gave clear and eloquent meaning to the correlations of ideal human body proportions with regard to sacred geometry. The figure of the Vitruvian Man was the principal figure of proportions in the classical order of architecture. It was a time, too, when poetry was introduced; just like the art of the human body this picture of the Vitruvian man represented this era as it was, what the picture of the inside represented to the eye. And it meant, too, to understand the concept of as within, as without.

Just like all Twins, this love means we would transcend the life we knew and understand life from a different perspective, a higher insight. It finds us here in the space of love, but it meets us in the most turbulent and transformative period of our life. This love changes us both in ways that would start from within, where love is felt the strongest: in the center, in the heart space, the center point of love. It was the like the Renaissance where romantic ideals began, as this was the time of literary evolution that evoked the mind's human nature of assimilation.

At this stage of life, romantic love is understood as a blessing, a gift of nature that one can celebrate and explore; the real, true essence of love is the legacy of who we were together. It is understood that this type of love is the rarest of loves...like the Renaissance era, this love evokes a new way of thinking as this becomes a manifest of written art, the story of revolutionized romantic love that is based on natural thought without holding back.

Our work would change as this, too, was understood as a transcendent aspect to our coming together and the conspicuous consumption of a tragic love story that gives meaning to a different sort of love, a love to be experienced, a love to be admired, a love to be sought after. It was like finding a perfect gemstone...one that is carved with the finest of details, to the exact fit, to every piece of insight of the pleasure of the other. It was in infinite desire that the recognition of the Twin Flame love was (and is) felt. However, this love presents its own contradictions, for with it comes sorrow and pain. Both would represent the greatest meaningful patterns we experienced, but this love story tells itself through the element of the art we make together, for it is a love of heavenly works and it is meant to be shared. It is to tell the story that allows this love to be set free, for it has no boundaries, only wings to fly.

With the spirit of the Renaissance comes a new thought of inspired free inquiry of creation; it is the Renaissance man, the square-in-the-box concept that awakens knowledge and thought. It is to delve into the thought of the mind of this time, the structure of thought like that of adopted ancient Roman architecture, the construction of the outside world, evolving from the thought of mind: one body, one mind. It represents the strong engineering and structures that have stood strong through the trials of lifetimes, an insight of basic Roman forms as they preferred arches and domes. It was here where classical order was introduced, and this is where the origins of assembly showed like that of the Twin Flame Divine Union. It was to look at a building's architecture and to know that the arch is the dominant decorative element. As it is with divine partnership, it meant to understand the dome was the mode that the classic building is akin to, as it is attuned to music in the raising of sound that resonates with its attuned audience. It is clear to know the harmonics that resonate with your own, as the sound of the heart is also understood this way.

Scene VII

I was sitting in my store and I texted London to say hello and he replied, "What are you doing?" I answered, "I'm just at the store and it's pretty slow today."

London said, "Me too. Not too many calls. Can I bring you Starbucks?" I told him that sounded great. He asked, "Same order?" I replied, yes, bring the usual. He showed up quickly, handed me my coffee, and asked if he could hang out. I looked at him, smiled, and said, "Of course."

He stayed and we talked while customers were shopping. When my last client left, he said, "Can I take you out for lunch?" I said, "Sure, that sounds nice." He asked if I wanted to walk to a restaurant nearby. I said, "I don't know downtown that well, but do you have somewhere in mind?" He replied, "Right across the way, there's a Greek restaurant. Let's go there."

I closed the store and we walked over. I'd never noticed this place, and as we walked in, I could see why he would choose this restaurant. It was homey and quaint.

He said, "Let's sit toward the back." I saw that we had people's attention, because he was in his police uniform. Slowly the background noise faded, and we started to talk. One thing I noticed that was different was that I seemed to make London a little uncomfortable. I wasn't sure why and I pretended not to notice.

I told him I'd never been to a Greek restaurant before, and that I wasn't sure what to order. He said, "Well, gyros are what they're known for, but they're pretty saucy...so you might like one of the plates."

I looked over the menu and decided on a chicken dish that came with jasmine rice and vegetables.

Lunch was pleasant, but I could tell London was trying to hurry. Once we were finished, we walked back and I expected that he was going to leave, but instead, he asked if he could come in. I said, "Sure, I thought you had to go." He said, "No, now I'll call in to take my break." I said, "I see." I opened the door to the store and let him in and closed the door behind us.

We walked to the back and I turned around to face him. I could see that his mood had changed. I saw that look of desire once again. I said, "Do we need to close the curtain?"

He smiled at this comment and said, "I think that would be a good idea." He pulled the black curtain closed behind him and walked over to me.

He picked me up intently and almost dropped me on my desk. Then he began kissing me eagerly. He put his hands down my shirt and under my skirt. Quite frankly, he took my breath away.

He was pressing down on me hard, but in his uniform, he didn't have a lot of liberty of movement, and we were trying to balance our weight against the desk at the same time. It didn't matter the obstacles. Our desire was undeniable. We wanted only one thing: We wanted each other.

I couldn't keep my eyes open and I couldn't keep them shut. I am in a fantasy—all about London—at this moment. All I could think in my mind was, "I need to catch my breath." I could hardly find air in this space. The appeal for the other was so real. Ravenous hunger for the other took over. He pulled my skirt up and moved my underwear.

I put my hands on his belt and unbuckled it and I can see him; he is so beautiful. I must put my hands to my face. I can't even finish what I'm doing for him below, and when I do, I feel how flushed I am, how flushed he makes me. The effect he had on my entire body was ambiguous. My mouth opened in awe and I breathed in and all I want is him, any of him, and all of him, all at the same time.

The mood was perfect. We were in heat for one other. He pulled down his pants. I couldn't believe that this was about to happen on our lunch break. Then, surprisingly, London's alarm clock went off, and he pushed off me. We were looking at each other, both of us breathing hard.

He pulled away and the look of his face changed, and I could read his face; he was looking at me like, "Who are you?" Frankly, I was looking at him and I was wondering the same thing. Who *was* London, and why did he make me feel this way?

I had to break the gaze between us because it was penetrating and uncomfortable. I looked away and as he was pulling up his pants, my eyes were drawn to his erection. I had to cover my mouth. I thought to myself, "Oh my goodness, he is huge and bulging out of his pants, literally."

I don't know why, but I started to laugh, and he gave me his crazy cop look and said, "What?" I said with a giggle, "Are you going to leave like that?"

He dropped his head to one side and said, "Do I have a choice?" He adjusted himself a little and left, just like that. This image of London, bulging out of his pants in his police uniform, would be an image that I couldn't get out of my mind for a very long time.

The Shadows

A new view overtakes our understanding of love and this benevolent fondness feels like a longing of consciousness. It awakens the soul with a love of unknowable depths and the muse of these emotions is a fluid acquaintance that was left in our imagination.

It is to experience the bare nakedness of being that captures the illusion and expresses the poetry of the heart through words. It is the synthesis of the emotional body, the moon and the sun, the ebb and flow of sentiment of poignant accolade.

To venture into our minds means to transcribe the feeling of Shakespeare's poetic magic…Shakespeare, the muse of human experience, thought, and words. The guild mind challenged and changed the mind of natural science, for it was Shakespeare's words that gave life to eloquence…the eloquence of passion, the nature of desires, the essence of the hungers, and the craze of the heart.

In the 16th Century, a change of thought emerged. It was the unconfirmed authenticity of words that took no credit of mind, for it was emotions alone that touched the heart of soul. It was the entanglement of emotions that captured the mind of romance and the element of the passions of love, but the unraveling of words transformed information through literature, coming from the ruminating desires that reflect the heavens.

In the comfort of fate, one saw only the truth of love. It was beyond the words of the constituents of love. Through love's tenacity, one could see despair, go into the deep, and find language of the greatest writer of all time, Shakespeare. It meant to go into the mind of inquisition, like that of the starry night, as only the stars give the essence of vision.

For it was our own hearts that fought us, leading us only to truth and the unveiling in the meaning of love. Reverence was not held to the constraints of our own beliefs, as love holds not to any boundaries, but it exists across all space and time. It does not hold to the elements, for the rudiments are only the radiance of the frequency that surround it. In the brightness of stars, one could see the true illumination of soul, that of the eroticism of passions of the heart, like the tarot of the wands and the element that creates the magic, coming from the desires of the foe.

It is to see the opposition...the side of love that holds to fear, the works of nature like that of the twin aspect: the face of pain, the shadows of death, the death of grief, the death of misery, the death of the soul's constraints. It means to go into solitude to consider what lays within the profound nature of one's mind, and let it be set free in the translation of innocence.

It is to shed away the layers of oneself, and then go where few people wish to venture, as one by one, the layers of the filter are unvarnished as you go deeper within the true nature of the purity of the nudity of the soul. To see things from the perspective of no time, for it was the time of soul that captured the mind of the tempest; time is an illusion and emotion connects it all. For it was from within to see the lights-camera-action dynamic, as it is the real stage inside the heart of matter. It is what makes the secrets of the mind expressed by scribe.

It is proficient thought, for it is the cosmopolitan culture that shifts understanding to what was, for the inside of the mind is like that of a desolate time of an envoy, a messenger. It is a state of mind... erudition, scholarship, life...the whole of it, our total involvement summed up in one thing, the link to it entirely: love, radiance and transparency, a manuscript of sacred flora. It is to bind the emotions of words with all the passions, the genius of the insight of the tarot of soul, the journey of sentiment. It is a time to transcend through words the expression of soppiness, the excess of tender feelings. It is to catch the mind of thought in the heart of spirit.

The discipline of the mind understands the beauty of art in words. It is in the heart's education that the emotion of metamorphosis is translated to classic romance. It is through the tale of plays that love, passion, truth, and violence move the audience.

It is the element of entertainment, the appeal of nudity, through plausible lust. It is the strength of words; it is the tearjerker gesticulation. In that talent lay the ability to tap into all things to ruminate one's true, natural reaction. The words culminate, buried in the mind of the beginning of a sonnet, the poetry of temperance. It is a poetic rival of an obsession, the fixation of the entanglement of love. It is this, an element of emotions, and all attachments of adoration bring a writer to the harmonics of music, where words and sentiment oscillate at a simultaneous frequency to bring about the translation, but to the duet of soul music.

It is to let go of doubt, and honor the soul instead, for this is the loyalty to self, well-regarded, with no logical constraints for these are the things not seen but felt. Love is always the driving force of all things, and the pressure of pure love of the heart is the driving force of the mind. The candles of light give rise to the idea of lust and illusions, the light of passion.

This mode of being means one would feel all the emotions. A sensitive person could not bear the nakedness this brought to the mind, the vividness of the reflection. What is love, but to feel, when all you can do is fall more and more for the element of love, the passion of lust becoming the possession of the mind. The passion set the core into a whirlpool as the hourglass falls into the nothingness of space, the element of the substance of everything.

It means to flee time, when time is no more, and the heart turns away. The heart falls in the constraints of the mind, for the two connect and the grip feels like a panting, that of the bellows of the voice of the heart. What are your darkest fears? The heart wants to ask this of the soul. The shadow of love, the shadows of the heart...the soul desires only the truth. It is the obsession of love, but following through to death, for it means to deal with the grief of the shadows and the element of change that needs to experience the darkest emotions of soul. In the darkness of the storm are found the noble thoughts of the mind, for the emotions are that of the deepest, most violent sea.

The experience means to deal with the dark, to see through the gloom. It is in the language of the visuals of all dimness that bring one to the place of understanding. It is to reverberate in the visuals of the mind. The ghost of the mind walks through the dreariness, and through the night one can see the light of day. It is the poet, the words, the magician who transcends the mind to connect to the heart. It was through the misfortune of the heart that one can find sorrow and the insight of courage. It is the mind's center, the symmetry of focus, the deep psyche of mind, the metaphor of life. It is the vivid nature of the mind's power to observe and transmute, thus connecting to the soul's depth. For it was in the darkness, in the deep of the abyss that the wavery feeling of fortitude over urge raids the heart as the ego fights to survive.

It is the heart that is left in desolation, for it is the purity of all substance, the acquaintance of the inner mind. It is to delve into the innermost core of the being, for the scariest of everything, all of it, lives in this abyss. It is a place in the mind of longing, the space between a thought. The desire of passion is the fascination of ponderance, of gravity and consequence, and the same reflection is that of a craze that will not allow reason to suffice the soul. It is only the idea of worship to the heart's ruminated desires that attach to the mind's imagination where the moral and immoral did not exist. It is doubted at times, but accepted in haze as the soul's truth, for it is the one thing that surpasses all else...the illusions of love, the rapture of thought, the all-consuming fire of the heart. There exists the reflection of suffering and longing of mind, the longing of the heart.

What is a tragedy, but that of a broken heart? It is to find the pieces in the inquest of the mind. To look at each fragile element and the wonder of thought that understands only the state of being, for it is in the brokenness of the bleeding heart where the emotions spill out. It is here where you can see an orifice of no depth, for it is the endless pool of blood that runs and in holding the heart, one can hear its voice.

It is Spirit's voice, for it is what withstood it all, the strength and the core of the being, the element of spiritual death. It is to find the source of the mind's exaltation, the reverence toward one's reality, and to find the answers to the queries regarding the most profound ideals of heart and of soul. It is to plainly see who is standing in the ruins of the darkness, for it is the light that captures the resilience of matter. It is the only thing that stands the test of time. It is to see behind the mask of darkness.

It is darkness that stands with light and it is the heart's magic, and it is the soul; it is to see the soul with nothing else, but the naked eye. It is the element of nothingness, for it is only light, the light of the dark of envy and solitude. It is the Will of life. It stands alone, the path illuminated, the rift of emotional connection to the light, the light of source that is illuminated in this time of obscurity. For obscurity is the muse of a new path, a pathway of tribute. It is a walk, a walk to light, and it is time for us to take our walk into the eloquence of light.

Scene VIII

London was enjoying another side that he has discovered in me: the fun, tipsy side of me after a few cocktails. This works well because he also likes his booze and the effect it renders. We are drawn to one another, not only for our pleasant conversations, but we have found something in each other that is just as stimulating, but a whole lot more exciting. We meet up at a restaurant again, and the conversation, as always, is fun and light-hearted, thought-provoking, and mentally stimulating. We always talked about random things, and it is refreshing, but primarily, we enjoyed each other's company.

We both know what this friendly, fun banter will lead to, because we are both very aware of what we've found in the other and in this connection. Because this is very much on both of our minds, we drink and have fun, but we wanted to move on to the more compelling component of this magnetically charged union.

We haven't been at the place very long, but we both felt our drinks and as if London could read my mind, he said, "Do you feel like going somewhere to sober up?"

I smiled at this, and I was wondering what he had in mind, but I was more interested in finding out, so I told him yes, I'd like that. This crazy attraction was something we couldn't hide. We couldn't even pretend to, because it was too distracting. It felt like we were two teenagers who had discovered sexuality for the first time, only I can never remember feeling anything remotely like this.

I said, "What do you have in mind?" He looked at me and said he didn't know, but let's find out.

We got into his car and he turned to me and says, "Can I take you anywhere?" I answered in the affirmative.

We didn't go very far. He found a building and parked his car behind it. He got out of the car and got in the back seat and closed the door behind him. I looked back at him and he said, "Come here."

I climbed over the center console to him, and he took me in his arms. He grabbed my legs, positioning me over him, and held my legs down with his hands.

He looked into my eyes and I had my head tilted to the side. He grabbed the back of my hair and pulled me to him. He kissed me so hard, I could feel pressure over all my senses. This hunger for the other took over completely. He began to touch me wildly everywhere and I allowed it all.

Quickly pulling each other's clothes off, we were enthralled in that moment. Realization then flashed over London's face. I looked at him, wondering what is wrong.

"I don't have a condom," he blurted.

I said, "You don't have a what?" He repeated himself and I almost wanted to laugh. I was disappointed, but I was mostly wondering why the hell he didn't have a condom. I said, "So, you didn't think we were going to have sex tonight?" He gave me a sarcastic look and said, "Well, I didn't know…" And I said, "*Really*, you didn't know?"

He stopped paying attention to the conversation as he began kissing me to shut me up.

I felt him pull my thong to the side and as he slipped inside me, I stopped paying attention to the conversation, too, and all my focus was on the pleasure of this moment. With London inside me, the feeling was ridiculously amazing. I could feel all of him. It felt so right, and so natural. We dissolved into the moment completely, and nothing else mattered. Everything just fell away.

That was the crazy thing about being with London…the overall and most distinctive feeling…that nothing else mattered. Nothing, no one, nothing else mattered.

We got lost in this fantasy world where the passion was so strong, beyond words or feeling or imagining. Our bodies dissolved into pure bliss. This was the first time I had made this distinct observation: It didn't matter where we were. The feeling would overtake us and we would dissolve into the essence of love.

Trust

It is the linguistics of art that gives rise to love in your language. It is the revelation of truth through the heart's rapture, to see things as they are construed. It is the piercing anointing of the golden arrow, the variance of signature of the undercurrent of the heart's domain, in a foreign presence, a nuance of the soul. It feels like a tide of lure, the unraveling of impression, and at the same time, the rise of munificence mixed with the ruins of transgression.

To be in this space means to see the heart, even the color of it, as it faces strife in its broken state. It is like looking and seeing your love, the equivalent of water spilling from the soul. There is nothing else the eyes can focus on because the eyes go astray. In the lapse of time, it is yearning you feel, made manifest. It is the thought, as the contemplation is what gives most meaning to the vision. It is to see the foresight that is in the mist, the mist over everything. It is the disheartening sorrow, the sadness that is indignant of all things; the feeling of blueness is the only thing that stands in the haze, as it lay under the wavering of sensation.

What is it to be in love? What is love? To understand love, one must understand all things in love are a rhetorical concept. Because it is always in tomorrow that you can see today. It is in the music's frequency as the music radiates into the atmosphere, and it comes back in the same frequency of today. What is the finiteness of life, if you consider the blackness? With love, and as in all things of love, it is color you see instead and a vision in your mind that brings the emotion of nature.

It is the imaginary illusion of love, for there is no rise that could not feel the hereafter of now. It is time, time for there is no more, only the tomorrow of it all. The bounds and the rhythm, the luminescence of time, as if with words there is a lack of meaning when there is no love. It is the pace of the day-to-day to look to tomorrow. What is time? And where do we record time, for the complexity of time is to see through all of eternity, and in love, we carry on. What is anything? The nothingness of it all, but the acolytes of time. For what is the oscillation of time when the core is seen as part of the whole, in the covenant of respite. It is the lull of the rapture caught in the heavens, like a haze overtaking the mind. It is an element of somewhere yonder, somewhere beyond, a restage of time.

As London and I got to know one other, it felt real, but it was of a different reality where love is the language, like a sheer fabric of prettiness, the transparent veil, wearing a color to reflect what is captured in the essence of space. It is the shawl that blows in the wind, for the wind of the tempered bleakness understands the air of significance. For in the time of falling, one would hold onto this emotion of love in order to bring the mind back to reality. Reality gives meaning to the emptiness that takes hold when the love is led to the vortex, a structure with no element to hold, as we fall into this... an unbridled feeling.

What is the concrete feeling of love, except what one feels? It is experienced like the mind snubbing and sneering at the heart, for the mind hears silence, but it cannot ignore the pleas of temperament that are felt over it all. The silence of the mind creeps in, the disposition of nothing, for here in the nothingness, all is absorbed in the significance of time. We learned not to fear time, as time is like dust, showing up in the shadow of existence.

Like the cobblestone beneath the feet that represents the path of life and brings the illusionary of time to light...light is in an eddy of fury, and the stone was a conductor of interval. As the ebb of fury turns the undercurrent toward the end of no day, it takes the night to find it. In the flood of ideals, you are akin to the knight of the suit of cups, for all the instinct of conquest brings one home to the flux of enchantment. It is to be in the streets of Rome, where you can physically visualize the radiance of enticement, where the elemental nature of the stone walkways give meaning to the Tiber banks of the soul's depth, for the vases that are lined over the doorsteps hold on to the imaginary love that is captured from within. Like rain captured within the vase, the true essence of the Great Mother, the water of life. The legendary root that flowers in the depth of the ocean of life, captured by the fantasy of mind.

What is it to sneer at the entity of time, for it is the dawning of day, to know the legends of fall, in the eyes of night like the hallow darkness seen in the vase, but when it is poured out, one sees the spilling of the contents within. All that live feel the chalice of all things, for it is in the mind that the element of emotions carried this, like the rapture of the ocean. These emotions are deeper than the guiles of oceanic gloom, a despondency of temperance. It is the duplicity of thought that was born, the cunning desires, for anything other than true love is the mind's deception.

Behavioral woes are a show of the ego of the baser mind, for melancholy reflects reality and represents nothing. It is nothing that cataracts the eyes and the soul's eye, and it is what is left in the despair of time, and all things left standing are of that of divine structure. I hear the soul cry out in respite. The ways of the ego mind are not the banquet; instead it is the feast of soul that is the ever-after, the treasures that live in the heart. The hunger that one feels is the hunt of the beast from within, but to know these things is to look deep and surrender, as one swims in the deepest oceanic tempest. It would be the flames of the fire that one finds, the scarlet of wonders, for it is the burn that scorns, in lust, to see the true ruby of the eye. The ego is feeble and in discord, for true strength dares one to shower in the flame, the purity of love's element, as most would curve the thought instead in order to avoid the countenance of fear.

It is the mind's intrigue that the justice of the polarity of discord finds a resolute ability to come to a colossal understanding. It is in the works, like a knight who comes out of the dismal, nocturnal sky, where it is in the wisdom of the inner truth that one is set free. It is a knight who comes from within, a hero of yourself, a hero of the higher, as it is the supernatural nature of the flight of mind. It is one's own mind, for it is to renounce the scholarly mind of self. It is in the recognition of one's own soul and in the understanding of the phantom of self, but it requires connection to know the layers of the face, the symmetric face. And it is to find that mask of each layer and peel it, page by page, only to find the emptiness underneath. It is to exist in the emptiness in order to find the cryptic understanding of all things, for the world will always wonder when the knight comes like a thief, as the pen is what gives meaning to all.

It is the playwright of the codes that one understands the meaning of life as we are manifesting what is in our minds, manifesting what is within. It is the symbolic view of all things. To understand ancient wisdom is to experience the compelling knowing of the ages, the veil of purpose of the rose and cross. It is to bring in science, religion, and mysticism, as it is the wisdom and the teaching of mystery.

In the nuance of intellect, it is the mystery that brings all things meaning. The mask of knowledge lay behind the shroud. It is the "do" time of all things, as it was to rise to the highest of the world and then to free-fall. It is a story of the emotions of life, the day-to-day climbing of the mountain and then, the opportunity to look back to see all the accomplishments, the grassroots of it all. It is the combination of the spiritual with the visceral, for who understands all the complexities when it is a battle of the base mind and the ego. It is to bring education, as most could not see beyond the veil of complete and total darkness when there is no spire to see on the surface of the open land. It is to break through the uncultivated land to Eden and the familiar tree of all acquaintance. It is a war of the roses, but what are the roses, but the fertility of life, the flower of life? It is in the flower the layers of what the fragrance brings to the mind, but it requires going into the mind to understand the scent. It is to peel the rose petal, layer by layer, to understand the communal knowledge that comes through in the primitive nature of thought.

It is to set the stage for all the world, and then to play the part. It is the heart that provides the manuscript. For the heart is full, and fully magnetized, and the shifts of the vision of desires that always find the oblivion of what is illuminated from within. What is it that sends the mind to the art of the color, rose? What is the mind's obsession, but that of the manuscript that reads like it was written by the scribe of all of time, like grains caught in the mist, and the immensity of it all, for there is depth that found no avail, only the color of prevalence.

Scene VIII

In this physical realm, London and I would often go out socially, which was a good way for us to be able to connect and spend time together. On this day, it was at a downtown pub. London ordered his regular drink, a Captain Morgan and a Coke. I also ordered my usual, a cranberry juice with vodka.

As we talked, London started to let me in on a man's perspective of women as he opened up about his feelings a bit. Feelings were something he didn't like to talk about, but this time, he did it in his own way. Of course, I was interested in learning more about him and his viewpoints, so he had my attention.

He said, "Do you know there is a scale that men rate women by?" I replied with a look of surprise, "Is that so?"

"Yeah, you see…we're all a little crazy, but there is a scale of crazy that men will tolerate women by," he said. I wanted to roll my eyes at him, because I wasn't sure what he was saying, exactly. He read my mind and nudged me on the arm and said, "No, look. I'm serious. Do you want to see?"

I smiled because I was irritated with him, but yes, I wanted to see. I wanted to know what he was trying to tell me.

He pulled out his phone, and he brought up a chart and showed it to me and said, "See? You are a unicorn."

I looked over at him and smiled. I could see that "unicorn" is the highest rating on the chart. I was very touched because London was giving me a compliment, and this was the closest I was going to get as far as revelations about his feelings toward me. So, I decided I would take what I can get. Even this early on, this was something I recognized that London didn't do. Feeling and expressing emotions … they were almost a foreign language to him.

Our conversation was interrupted by a phone call from my oldest daughter. She was babysitting the younger kids and was having issues at the house. At the time, truth be told, there were supernatural occurrences going on all around me, with my house and my whole family. It was if we had a dark cloud that had formed over us, a sort of evil storm. My daughter was a bit panicked on the other end of the phone and said she witnessed something very strange and she wanted me to come home. I asked her to call Sam, as he was at our house at the time. She said he was at the store and would be back soon.

I got off the phone and London looked at me with a questioning look: "Who's Sam?"

London and I were and are very open, naturally open, with each other. I said, "Oh, he's my first ex. He's like a brother to me now and to make a long story short, he's been in my life since I was 17. Now he's like family."

London didn't even have a verbal response except, "Ahhh…"

Then he followed up with, "So what's he doing at your house?"

I said, "That's a long story." I realized I had said the wrong thing as soon as it came out of my mouth.

I looked at him and I had his full attention, but I didn't want it, in this case. London was looking for an answer, but I didn't have one because it would have required me to reveal too much.

But I could see that he wasn't going to let me escape this moment. Since I was drinking and didn't feel I had anything to hide, I told him the truth.

"Sam is in town visiting, and he usually stays over when he's in town."

London broke eye contact and started staring off into the distance straight ahead of him. He did this thing where he puts his tongue over his top teeth, and he was doing this as he was processing the information. At that moment, I knew, without a doubt, that I dropped in ranking on his chart. In fact, I think I dropped off the chart altogether.

This moment would be the start to our battle. This revelation put him on high alert, and he began to test me. Ugliness became a part of this relationship, as trust became our enemy.

The Test

What was it, in the avail of nothing, the simplicity of wit, to see the structure of time? For in the abyss of such thought gives the rise of the mind's ability over the feeling to be in awe, as one ponders the consideration, as the void of disheartenment gives way to the docile surrounding, that of the footsteps of mediumship to spirit.

It is in the quiet of the mind, the ability to seek what comes from within, but the real knowing comes from an understanding of where the thought comes from. It would come to the knowing, in the development of connection to self this power, for the divination of time synchronizes, to the fields of the outer mind's realms, as these coincide to serve as the purviews of guile*. It was the expression of Old English that surmounts the call of prevail to the cleverness as to allow what is to just be. Consider that, in the framework of all things, there is hidden meaning in the context, of the core; for what so grounded our physical body to the earth, there serves a purpose as to the origins, as to explain a mystery of basis. That of the sacred tree of life that gives rise to all the legitimacies of the feelings for the understanding of legacy to the other.

It is the complexity of thought, as it sends us in the continuum of the atmosphere around us, to find precision. In alignment with our higher Will, it is only in the honoring of the feelings that is the answer of authenticity, for there is no other reality but the heart. For it is in the heart, the secret wisdom, the single most transparent element in all the body. It is the conductor of energy that holds everything else in functional substance. It is the single element alone that serves as

---

* *Guile: Sly or cunning intelligence.*

the serenity to the soul, the calm to introversion, the connection of within.

By way of understanding the works of Shakespeare, it is the connection of words to infinite space and through the telegraph, as he once quoted, "the inaudible and noiseless foot of time." For many of his references made connection of the sky, the heavenly sphere of ideas and thought, and the connection of all things to the Sun, Moon, Stars, Comets, and the Eclipses of cosmology.

It is the thought of reason further linked to Galileo for his fascination and study of the topic, with his innovation of thought and what is seen through the lens of his telescopic discoveries. What is in the consolation of the stars, the heavens on ponders, for what lives in the ideal of thought, as these are the surmount of the formation of these things, the intellect and the ability to find reason? The mystical thought, where does the configuration of structure come from, other than that of mysticism, the frequency of the alignment of idea with a motif? It is the configuration of all the solar system, that lends promising acquaintance as the stars speak their brilliance to us. For it is through discord that inquisition was threatened. But it is physics in its birth that shows the beauty of the connection of the stars and love. It is astronomy that shows the passion of nature, for it is through the eyes of passion that one understands such things. It is to see further than common thought and limitations and to heed this was to go beyond to see all else clearly, as all comes together to evoke the imagination.

For the creation of all was God's work. The stars of thought transcend the ability to see this in the clock and almanac of macroevolution. For it is the chain of this world that links all matters. It is the mathematical mind, the universal language of the world, the triangle, the circle, all the geometric figures that give meaning to one of the other, that give correlation of each to the other, as it is to see sacred geometry that will give rise to the technique of thought for a foundation of reflection.

It was the ambition of scholarly wit, for the novelty of spectacles gave the new eye. It was through a tool; it was a magnified glass that yielded the optics of illusion. It was to reshape the magnified glass; his telescope would give rise to the reshaping of the insight of cosmology, and of thought. It was a spy glass that would give a view of the bigger scope of life, the illumination of the sky and all the secrets that held meaning and reason.

Scene IX

After our last date, the text messages between London and I have changed. I would usually receive a text from him that said, "Hello" or "Good morning," but this morning, I didn't.

The day whiled away, and I was wondering if he was upset, so I sent a text that said, "Hey, good afternoon."

I receive a text back: "I'm not having a good day."

I can sense where this is going, but I kind of walked into this as I asked him what's wrong. He told me that his pipes had burst at his house, and that he didn't want to talk about it. He said he would text me later.

I respected him and waited until later, but then I texted to ask: "Is everything okay?"

He replied with a one-word response: "Yes."

I asked if I could call him. He said I could, but he wanted me to know he wasn't in a good mood.

I thought talking to him, instead of the back-and-forth of text would help, but I came to find out he is true to his words. London is the type of person who you really don't want to talk to when he is in a bad place; he had told me that about himself before.

And now I could see why. As I was talking to him, he started lashing out at me for no reason.

I asked if I could see him. I don't know why I did that, because it just made him angry.

He said, "Look, I didn't want to talk. I told you that. And in fact, I don't want to talk later either. And I definitely don't want to see you because I'm in a bad mood."

This is his reason, so I don't question it. In truth, I was a bit hurt, but I respect his request and his space.

I learned the lesson about taking London at his word, as he is quite a literal person. My goal was not to pay too much attention to all of this. In truth, I almost wanted to pretend to not see this side of him, but this was only the beginning of seeing the other side of him, only a glimmer of the other parts of London.

The next day, I received a "good morning" text from him, just as if nothing had happened. He asked if I wanted to go out that evening and he suggested we watch a movie at his house. I said, that sounds nice. But then I asked him if he wanted to go out to dinner first or out for drinks.

He replied, "Yes, let's do that. Why don't you come over and we can go somewhere close to my house?" When we walked into the restaurant, we bumped into a few of his buddies. He said hello to them and asked if he could introduce me. I replied, "Sure."

We walked over and he introduced me to two guys, telling me that they worked together at the police department. The guys exchanged a few jokes. We walked over to the bar and London started to tell me about one of the guys. He said he was his partner on the police force when they first started and there had been an incident. I listened to him tell his story and I was thinking that it was respectable of him to tell me something so intimate and personal and despite the sadness of the story, I was glad he was entrusting me with the details of his life.

We ordered drinks and he ordered something for dinner. He asked if I would like to eat something, but I declined because I wasn't hungry.

Overriding me saying I wasn't hungry, he said, "I'm ordering a steak and you're going to eat some of it." But I didn't argue with him. When London received his plate, I watched as he cut his steak up, and I was surprised by what he did next. He took a piece of steak and dipped it into a sauce and held it up for me to take a bite.

I smiled at him and I ate the steak from his fork. I closed my eyes and savored the flavors, enjoying what was in my mouth. In my mind, I was thinking of this kind gesture and I was touched by his intent and the fact that he thought of me first. He finished eating and pushing his plate away, he said, "What do you want to do now?

I said, "I thought we were going back to your house to watch a movie?" He turned to me and said, "Well, I thought we could do something besides have sex." My mouth opened and I was taken aback by his comment. I was thinking "How dare you?" and so I said, "Are you fucking with me?" loudly.

He didn't like the attention we drew, so he said, "It's okay. Let's go back to my place, but he was clearly irritated.

I was trying to figure this all out in my head. I was confused. We came here to be close to his house so we wouldn't have to drive far, and what did he just say to me? How could he put that on me, as sex was a very mutual thing between us? I thought to myself, "What the hell is going on?"

We got to his house, and I didn't even know if I wanted to be there. I wasn't ready to drive home, though, as I was still tipsy.

He said, "Let's watch it in my room." He made some popcorn and picked out an 80s film. The mood settled a bit and he was telling me something about the movie. He stopped the conversation in its tracks, though, and then out of nowhere, he said, "Do you know you make me very uncomfortable?"

I was feeling perplexed. London had long made it a habit to confuse me with his words and senseless antics, so I looked to his face for some clarification. I then asked my famous question: "What do you mean?"

He said, "Exactly what I said. Did you not hear me?"

London said it again, but slower this time. "You ... make ... me ... very ... uncomfortable!"

The expression on his face was somewhat amusing, as he was mad and even dropped his popcorn on the bed. He stood up, then, and once again said: "Yes, you make me feel awkward."

I wanted to say I am sorry, but I didn't even know what I should be sorry for. Instead, I say, "London, what are you talking about?"

I feel like I'm on a Seinfeld episode, but this is real life. I was trying to be compassionate about his feelings, and I honestly didn't understand what he was saying to me.

He followed it up with: "Do you need me to explain to you how you make me feel awkward?"

I said, "Yes, please do." But now I've made him angry. He was glaring at me. He said: "The way I act, the way I talk, the way I feel around you. It's not how I normally act, talk, or feel. YOU make me feel awkward," and it was like he was spitting these words at me. He looked like a kid throwing a fit.

I didn't know how to respond to this, much less what to say.

I almost thought the whole scene was cute and I felt like I just wanted to hug him and to tell him it was okay. I wanted to laugh and say, "Are you joking with me right now?" But mostly, I thought about how sweet it was that he was sharing his feelings and being honest and open. Clearly, he was mad, though. I am not sure where his anger was coming from, as I didn't do anything to deserve it. So, I couldn't play the "I understand and thanks for sharing" card right then, as it would only make him angrier. I stood there, wondering what he wanted me to do.

Undoubtedly, we have entered a different stage in this relationship. It was the stage of reflection, what he had intuitively noticed and what he was describing as awkward was all his inner feelings surfacing. It was the process of looking into a mirror of oneself. It was a feeling of that person looking back at you and they see inside of you, all of you.

It brings a feeling of understanding that you cannot hide anything from the other person because they can feel these things, too, and see things they're not supposed to see, but they do.

All your inner secrets are revealed, things you don't like to admit or even acknowledge. All a person's deep secrets are uncovered and revealed by the other's reflection.

This would be the very beginning of this process, the unfolding of this journey, but later in this relationship, this concept would take a completely new meaning as our emotions became involved and as we became more comfortable around each other. This is when this relationship began to show its true face.

As our souls connected, we began to cross over into a different realm of understanding each other. We begin to reflect on things from the inside. There was, and is, a great deal of pain attached to this process as one is forced to bring all these things that are going on in the inside—things that are deeply suppressed and rooted—to the surface. As this process is taking place, our relationship is formulating on a different level of understanding.

London was looking at me in the eyes and expecting me to understand what he was talking about, but I really didn't, at least, not yet. When he saw that I didn't have words, he said, "I think you need to leave." My head dropped to the side with disappointment and I let out a deep breath. I wanted to give him space and I needed to process all of this in my head, so I let him walk me to the front door.

But London wasn't finished with confusing me on this night. He was convinced I hadn't seen enough of "ugly" yet, and "ugly" wanted to have some fun with me tonight. As we were walking through the dining room, he let his dogs in. We got to the front door and he reached over and picked up the doggy bag he had brought back from dinner: His leftover steak. He opened the bag and pulled out the piece of steak, holding it high above his head, and called out to his dogs.

The dogs were all over me right now and as I petted them, he said, "Little bitch, come here."

I was looking down as I was petting the dogs, but then I shifted my eyes to him. He got my full attention as my body was shocked into an upright position. I looked at him and I found his eyes, but I didn't have an expression. Honestly, I didn't even know where my mind went at that moment, but we then held each other's stare. I recognized what he was doing. He was testing me, but this was a very heinous way to do it. He was still holding the steak above his head and the dogs ran over to him.

He was still looking me in the eyes, and he started to curse his dog out, while he looked at me. I had no words for him; I didn't even react. He continued this for a while, and noticed I just stood there, almost frozen, but that I wasn't going to play into this.

One thing he didn't do—he couldn't do—was phase me and insult me. Really, he didn't do anything except make me wonder what the hell was wrong with him.

Clearly, I knew he was testing me, but what kind of test was this? What I was starting to see was that I was often like a receptacle to his nastiness. He finally gave the steak to the dogs and petted them and started to coo at them. He looked over at me and said, "That was pretty cool. I can curse like a sailor and you don't even react."

I have no words, and I frown because my mind really didn't understand how to process such nonsense, but at the same time, it understood that this was something else, but what was it?

I know now that London was testing my feelings for him. He was beginning to understand that he could act any way, do anything, say anything, and it didn't scare me, or make me not want to be with him. He understood from his little test that he couldn't make me leave, he couldn't change my feelings for him, and he couldn't change this state of affairs. It simply was what it was.

Storm of Emotions

It is in the storm of emotions, when one looks into the eternal knowing. It is then that one could break through the fear as the desire to know is from a different place, as it is the core of one who wants the answers. It is the desire for knowledge as a lifetime of grief will not suffice the mind's need for the heart's treatises. It is to look at the fundamental work of Aristotle and to see the logic of reason, for the perception of all knowledge comes from our senses. It is to look at something and identify that the properties of what is looked at is through the perception of one's eyes to interpret such things as love and beauty, for it is through the abstract universal entities that attractiveness is preserved. It is to contemplate the knowledge of why one thing to one is what it is to another. Is it still something more? Is it to know this instead through the primitive mind; is it to know this through the eyes of the soul?

Will you recognize me...will you know me...will you remember? I hear my heart plead, but I ask who is it that you plea to, who is it that hears these cries? So, the heart cries anyway and cries and pleas for there is an understanding of the perceived wonder of the illusion of you. How is it to connect to such things? How is it to reach out and understand where these instinctive ideas live? For it is only the soul that understands and responds and says, yes, for all things relate to art, the art of your soul; it is the colors and the wonders that coincide with such things. As these things cannot exist apart from that with which it has a relation. It is the math of the mind, $1+1=2$; an idea is then also attached to a knowing, a memory, a connection of the past, for the soul reaches to understand the mathematics that are not of focus to the mind, for the frequency needs to be in the right plane to appreciate such logic.

Scene X

I was in court and dealing with a lot of things in my life, and I needed a distraction today. That was who London had become, in a way: my personal distraction. The fantasy we found in each other, something beyond my wildest dreams, had come true. The pleasure, the seductive aspects of it, was the most auspicious love affair one could imagine. All I had to do was call him and tell him I needed a distraction and he knew exactly what I meant and exactly how to give it to me. He knew how to take my mind off of all my problems. Only he could give me what I wanted. The problem became the more I got of him, the more I wanted. The forces that brought us together like magnets are too strong. Our relationship intensified, but here is the other problem, everything seems to intensify with it. Not only did the sex get more and more passionate, seductive, unbelievable, and undeniable, but the arguments and the pain were taking on a new, heightened level, too. To put it into perspective, it felt like the best sexual experience of your life coupled with extreme lows, with the fights starting over nothing and being insignificant, but these arguments would blow up in our faces.

A conflicting mix of emotions brewed inside of me and the aftermath of it was hard to bear. I would question how something that was so incredibly perfect could feel so petrifying at the same time.

But London wanted me to come over and have coffee today and I headed over to his house. He greeted me at the door and welcomed me in.

"It's hot in here. I'm going to leave the door open," he said.

He invited me to the dining room, motioning for me to sit.

"We can talk a little if you want," he said. He seemed to be in a good mood, and I was grateful to see him.

"Sure," I said, with a smile, and I sat down.

I told him about my court date and how things went. London offered some helpful advice: "You see, with your ex, it's all about control if you're trying to understand what he's doing."

I said, "Okay, I guess that makes sense."

He started to have a rather long conversation with me about how men like to control women and that this man was going to control me and every aspect of my life if I let him. He looked at me and said, "You need to take back control of your life."

I said, "What do I do? Do I start writing down all these things that are going on around me and report it to the police?"

"No, people will think you're crazy," he replied.

I asked, "Then what do I do?"

He said, "You take control; you don't give up control."

He looked at me with those eyes and I could tell what he was thinking. I smiled because I already knew what he wanted. He asked me to come to him and I did, and he reached up as I was standing in front of him. He put his hands over my face, pulling me down to him, and he started kissing me.

He took off my jacket as we continued kissing. I could feel him put his hands on my hips and he picked me up and sat me on his dining room table. I was looking around and I was thinking, "Really, *here?*"

I noticed the door was still open, and then I looked at his face, and as if he had read my mind, he said, "Yes, here."

My mouth opened a little and I said, "What if your Mom comes? Or one of your exes, or anyone?"

And London said, "Well, then, they'll see something they don't really want to see, but that's not our problem."

I had to laugh at his logic.

He wasn't really paying attention to my words at this time. I was wearing a dress and he had pulled my dress up as far as he needed to. He was wearing his gray shorts he wore the first time I met him for the jog.

I saw him put his hands in his shorts, pulling himself out, and then I saw all of him. And then I felt him, and I was in this high, this high of London. He was so passionate in the moment, and he just watched me enjoy him until he couldn't take it anymore, and then we were done, right there, yes, right there on the dining room table.

The Roadmap to Unconditional Love

It is a compass of the soul, a roadmap, if you will, to the connection of what makes us who we are to understand through the lifetimes of reincarnation, through the memories and perceived ideas that the mind brings into focus, but only for the precision of an attentive soul. It is to understand higher logic, as it is to understand higher love that comes from cosmic consciousness. It is to question reality, and further to look at our own existence, but then to look at the presence in the basis of our genetic makeup of time, the immortal soul.

It is to put into practice these ideas to make it real, for happiness is to find the question that will get the answer. In the conception will be to find how to pursue such an idea, for the mind seeks to find the feeling associated with love. What is the root of love then, as the root is the core to understanding? The concept is the one of what is home. For it means to become whole. It is the understanding of what makes us, as the desires of the heart. All things come from actions, and the actions that are from the heart are the actions that will allow you to make the right choice. It is a thought that comes from the heart. It is honor. And it is honor of self that praise and esteem come from within.

It is the pleasure of the heart, for the heart is the center of pleasure, but it is to know what this feeling is. For it is to find the pleasures, the ancient understanding of pleasure, that will shed light on love in the cerebellum of the brain. It is through the works of scribes that one can pass on the shrewdness of candor. It is the acumen with which one would become attuned to the reality of time.

Ones' time of reason—in the reason that surmounts the canniness that is seen in the eyes of eloquence—it is the kiss of the power of deliverance of the ego's infringements, for it is to find the soul's expression. It is to do the soul dance of the Twin Flame to understand this, as it is to honor that dance of the soul and always live by this knowing, the knowing of coming home. It is a deliverance of injustice, as liberation of the soul: the flower child from within, that of all of time in the connection to all of time.

It is to learn from the master of logic, to exhibit sagacity as it relates to love. It is the individual understanding, as all things are to reason through oneself. It is the equation: Reason equals virtue equals happiness. It means to let go of all the mind's constraints, to give way to the logic of intellect. It is the visceral world that lends a wave of the concept formation of the truth. It is the magic of the mind, as the philosophy of the mind that needed to overcome and believe in the mission. It is in the virtue through that of the suit of wands, to know what it is to know…the soul level of understanding. For, as it is through knowing, that during time…secret associations and secret eruditions of learned atonement, as it would be in the action through true heart-rending of the discipline of works, as to the art of all things, the conquest that brings back the argument of an oratorical thought.

As the heart's spirit surges never-endingly, it is the ability of spirit that could find the work of life, where the mind's logic kicks in, for the heart needs to live on to the aspiration of validity. It is in life that one will find the path, the higher way to the celestial. It is in the divine, for the understanding of Gem, the mind, is the sword of truth. It is the knowing of the deliverance and of the message that one could not only send, but also conceal in meaning. It is to sin against philosophy for the mind, and then to just let it all go, as it was too difficult to know.

What was in the skills of all things, as knowledge is always to be hidden, for it is in the pain of erudition, of scholarship, that the dark of the mind's premises would one want to know. For the treasures are to enlighten the soul, as this is the synthesis of ideals in the mind, for the degree of knowledge will be to merge truth with a formulaic sense. It is to ask the question, and here is where the barrier comes in as the mind and the truth hold an impediment. It is here to see consciousness, for logic is in dominance of individual thought, but it would need to be here where one changes this instead, to ask the question, when you know the question. It is here where you could ask your heart and say...the aspiration is what you long for, but what is it that you plea, what is it that you covet, what is it that brings you happiness? The heart answers with just one word. It is the most peaceful of all feelings to hear the heart, whispering in the most beautiful voice as the eyes of the soul find me and respond: "Love."

Scene XI

The energy around us had clearly changed and was quite drastic. In this shift, what I saw was that London was having a hard time expressing his feelings toward me. I felt the strongest urge to communicate to him what he meant to me. So one day, I said to him, "Can I send you a letter?" I really wanted to let him know what I was feeling, and I thought a letter would help him understand. But he said, "No, I don't want you to send me a letter." I asked London if I could see him. I wanted to talk about my feelings, as I didn't understand what was happening, why I kept feeling this pull, and why he wasn't being clear with me either. But London was scared of this topic; in fact, it terrified him. I wanted to talk, though. I needed to talk, even though "feelings" was not something he wanted to discuss. But in some ways, I felt like I was going to make him tell me his truth.

I was irritated and a bit suspicious of his actions and I wanted to talk with him. I asked if we could meet for coffee. He said, "Well, I'm working from home right now, but you can come over if you want." Our text messages had become a back-and-forth, push-and-pull and I wanted to understand. I had questions for him because things were not making sense.

I got to his house and brought him coffee. He walked me over to his dining room and we sat at the table. We started to talk. I said, "You've changed with me and I want to know why."

He looked up from the table and had a smirk on his face. He said, "I can't give you what you want." I was taken back by his comment and I looked to his face because this answer wasn't going to be sufficient in my mind.

I said, "London, you completely led me on, and now you are going to sit here and tell me that you can't give me what I want, when you *are* what I want."

He said, "I didn't lead you on."

"Of course you did. With your actions and your words."

He said, "I always told you the truth and I said, 'Let's see where this goes.'"

"You're not going to play this game with me," I said. "From the very beginning, you led me on, and now you're going to pretend like all of this never happened, like it was a joke."

He said, "Tell me how I led you on."

I said, "Look, I'm not here to waste my breath. You **know** how you lead me on. It's what you've done now that I'm more concerned with."

"What do you want?" he asked.

I said, "I just want to understand."

"I'm telling you I can't give you what you want," he said.

"So, London, are you telling me that you just used me?" I asked.

He looked at me and said, "What?"

I said, "You heard me, because if you're saying you don't want to pursue this, that's basically what you did: You used me for sex."

He said, "What do you want from me?"

"Excuse me. What I want to understand is what's going on? Tell me why things have changed," I replied.

He looked at me and said, "What, do you want a roadmap to me?" I felt like his words slapped me in the face.

Now his mixed messages are starting to make sense to me. He was callous and insensitive. Frankly, I felt he was heartless. What he was doing was saying something and leading me on, but then his actions didn't match his words.

I pointed this out to him and told him he was being evasive. He didn't like what I was saying to him, and he started to dance around my words.

London is highly intelligent and will not allow himself to get caught in a lie, so he was using his police tactics on me.

He pushed my buttons and I said to him, "Look, London, when I met you, you were working, and you asked me out. You weren't supposed to do that."

He responded, "Says who?"

I said, "You were on the job and you basically asked me out. Then you used me for sex and now you're telling me you're all done with me after you used me. Do you not see something wrong with this picture?"

"Look, I was helping you and you were the one who seduced me," he said.

I said, "*WHAT?*"

He said, "You were the one who asked me back to my room."

At this point, I was so over-the-top insulted by him and I said, "I wasn't asking you to have sex with me. I wanted to watch a movie."

He said, "*Really?*"

I said, "Oh, of course, **really**. I didn't plan to have sex with you. You kissed me."

"No, we kissed each other," he said.

I took a step back, realizing who I was dealing with, someone was very good at twisting the truth and manipulating a situation. I was very impressed by his tactics, but my mind was too outraged and offended by his words to reflect on his mental abilities.

He saw that he had very thoroughly offended me, and he used another of his tactics, one of his "cover-all" phrases. He said, "It all comes down to your perspective on things."

I wanted to scream. I knew I would not win with him, not today.

He looked at me and said, "Hey, come here."

I said, "What?"

He said again, "Come here."

I swallowed hard, and I went over to him. He pulled me down to him and had me sit on him, crisscross, on his dining room chair and he started to kiss me. That was all it took. His kiss made everything else go away. This is what he did to me. This fantasy of London made everything go away: Every problem, every truth, every worry. He stood and held on to my legs and wrapped them around him as he walked me to his room. He started kissing my neck and laid me down.

He started to take every article of clothing off my body, one by one, and then he got his sheet and put it over me.

He whispered in my ear. "This here, this is for you," and he grabbed my hand and put it over his erection.

He said, "I know how you like to be satisfied. You like to be on top and I want you on top today."

He got undressed and let me watch him. He said, "Let me get underneath you."

He continued, "I want you to feel this, and I want you to take control today and I want to watch you. I'm not going to do anything. I want to watch, and I want to see you get there." I was so seduced by his words.

"Can you feel me?" he asked. I nodded my head. He said, "I want you."

"Grab me and put me inside of you," he said. "I want to be inside of you."

I do as I'm told. He said, "I know you're a good listener and you like to do what I say. Look at me."

And I did look at him, but my eyes were in ecstasy at that moment.

He said, "Can you feel me inside?" I looked at him and I was biting my lip. I could hardly stand it. The feeling of him was mind-blowing.

"I can see how much you're enjoying yourself," he said. "Feel this. Feel the moment. Slow, slow, make this last."

My mind is in a sort of a high from London and his voice was only getting me higher. I enjoyed taking his instruction and I didn't want anything more than I wanted him at that moment, and he saw it.

As I looked at his face, he had a half-smile on, and was studying my expression and right before I got there, he sat up and grabbed my hands, and put them behind my back. He held them there with one hand, taking his other hand to grab my hair, lightly pulling on it. I let my body fall back.

He couldn't keep still anymore, and he started to work me. He got me there and I just looked at him, thinking, "How is this even real?" My head fell all the way back and I just enjoyed that moment as my body submerged into his ecstasy. I started wondering at that moment, "Who is really using whom?"

He put his hand to my face and brought me back and said, "My turn...flip over."

I laughed, and I did as he asked and he patted me on the butt and said, "Come on."

I turned my face to look at him and he grabbed my hair and he said, "I need you to come up to me." I knew what he meant, and I did and then he was inside of me again. Now I watch him, as it's his turn.

Push and Pull

What was it to the mind...to understand the conquest of time? It would be through love. So, I ask myself the question again, what is it to fall in love? I use this as a meditation tool to reach deep inside myself for answers. I understand it would be in my soul where I could find such erudition, such understanding, but I also know this is an answer that will come in season. It will be a measure of the heart that would be like a compass, for it was in my focus to search for the liberty of poetic justice. It was my own personal vow to Self that I would find this realization; it was my promise of love to my own soul to comprehend this from the view of the Divine.

In lifetimes of trajectory, it means to ascertain human principles, those passed on and brought into view in linear time, from ancient philosophy. It means to understand the mind more fully in connection to soul, and our own wants of human nature. As with Socrates who possessed a brilliant mind and was Plato's teacher, one could see unified ideas of identified philosophy of abstract thought. It is nowadays just a matter of study, but to him and his time, it was to know philosophy as a way of life, to truly understand it as a heightened sense.

Philosophy was art, in the dialectic gift for enduring thought that would enrich the ethics of self. The question being then, who is self? For is it inside where the self lives or is it outside...the portrayal of the picture of self that one paints. The comprehension of self was the conquest of study, for the character of a person was the rhetorical question, for it was the structure of within, as it was one's perception from within that should reflect the without. However, does one truly know the self? For it was then to consider morals that of polarity and dichotomy of the darkness and light, the feminine and masculine, and the employments of the brain and rational thought. What was someone's conception, for it was brought on by the circumstances of life; however, who is to judge this, and by which criteria are we judging?

It means to understand the self in a more thorough way of knowing, for the senses of one's own divine knowing is thus meeting of the mirror that shows us all things that were true, within. It is here where you meet your Twin. It is here where the light of day is reflected with a magnifying glass from within; the optical illusion is theologically blinding, as it is to give a shining reflection of the wisdom that lies within. For it means one would look at all things, through all of life, and with life, it is to be in the circumstances…to know. What is called instinct—a matter of survival—the consciousness of reacting in a situation…what one does and doesn't do, is it given to situation or was it given to the mind of logic or our own will? It is inherently that one responds, or is it conditional, as this is further related to the construction of a situation and is this more so related to the structure of one's self?

This relationship felt so conflicting, the push and pull, the cross of conflict, and because we did not understand, we let blame become our game. The conclusion I arrived at was that we just were not able to accept what this was; we did not know how to process the entirety of it. However, we had the one thing that kept us coming back for more, because it was the connection that had our attention.

Scene XII

London and I decided to meet again for lunch as he was on his lunch break from work. He talked about his shift and what he had going on. Then he said he had to go home to check on his dogs before he went back to work.

So, we got up and left the restaurant and walked outside. Before he left, he turned around and we looked at each other. London verbalized, "Come here so I can give you a hug."

I went over to him, wrapping him in an embrace, allowing his warmth to permeate my soul. I smelled his neck as we held each other, and smelled his warm, musky smell. This aroma never eluded me; it was the fragrance of home.

Whenever I was with him in the moment, he was such a beautiful person to me. I always felt like I was fantasizing in my own fantasy world, like I could just stay wherever I was and stare at him forever. It was this same understanding that snapped me back to reality and the realness that I could only temporarily see him this way because the minute I thought, "Maybe this could last a while," was the same minute that London would show me his other side. The endless cycle of confusion continued.

I got in my car and I couldn't move as I thought about this, the crazy effect that London had (and continues to have) on me. All it took was his embrace to take me to places in my mind that I had never been. As I was thinking about this, I began to have a recollection of an instance with London, one that I didn't like to reflect on, because it was a disheartening feeling that I don't like to remember.

It was the feeling of rejection that his sometimes thoughtless ways would leave on me, a difficult memory to revisit. But the embrace in this moment took me back to it.

God's Will

For what Will is it that speaks to this, for is it here to see divine Will or God's Will? What are the circumstances of life as a whole, for these are the experiences set forth before us, for is it not based on actions completely? Is it, I ponder, based on the mind, the thought, the understanding of the depth of the soul and the connection to reality, nature, and the illusion and visualization of art as it is in the screenplay of our life? Through the divinity of Twin, one would find the conquest of self, in order to see the mirror of soul.

For it is with the reasonable understanding of antiquity, the capability of the soul to understand ancient love. It is to understand one from the root of affection, to know that this is the way, as it is the conquest of light the strongest and truest reflection of within. It is from within that would bring the art and discipline, for it is to reach the art of logic, to understand the mind, the attachment to thought, and the nature of the mind, as the divine nature is what the mind finds. This is what yields self-satisfaction when one is true to self and the soul.

It is to honor one's own scribes of the heart. It was to understand the self, when you allow the constraints of modern ideas of polarity, the right and wrong, for it was in the bases of consciousness to know, as with that of your inner fortitude to permeate these notions and retrieve them from within. This is precisely what will bring the satisfaction of spirit: the notion of self-rediscovery.

It is to recognize the study of nature, that of the divine: where one could find this art from intimate, esoteric scholars. It is to meditate on the eternal allusion of self. It is here to see the divine structure and to further find the heart's scribe. It is in the path of life that one finds the soul's path, for the divine is the higher consideration, the undying. It is engraved on the emphatic soul, the dialog of the way of life. It is like a pattern of tradition, a mere custom that one etches authority of the core.

It is the explication of the discussion of compassion, for it is the heart's philosophy that one would have to tame, in order to command control—for justice of the heart—the rhetorical skill that seeks to understand the logic and anchor it to the tenderness of self-harmony. For it is the spirit and the soul's condition that is of most importance to balance, for it is in the walk of the soul to the grounding of this acquaintance, above all else. It is to see that this is the unconditional of all other conditions, as it is the whole of the soul that sets one free to all indifference. The soul is the eternal connection to life's virtue, as it is in the soul where all things triumph the wretchedness of strife.

Scene XIII

I began to feel a big pull. There's a distinct change and I was trying to figure out what had happened. I was beginning to realize that I was falling in love. I didn't recognize it by these words, only that London was always on my mind and when he started to pull away, the effect this left on me reignited somewhere deep inside. I sensed that, in a way, he was being dishonest, or that there was something else, some other reason as to why he was pulling away. He kept coming up with excuses of why he couldn't get together at that moment, or why he didn't want to be involved and once I received this revelation and confirmation that he didn't want anything serious with me, I was crushed. I didn't understand and I needed to understand.

I clearly remember there was a big shift that took place with London, and at this point he completely pulled back. This was the same time I was beginning to realize I had fallen in love with him.

Our conversations via text had become very distorted. It felt like we were constantly fighting, and I was wondering why this was happening. I wondered whether there was someone else and what made him change his heart so much. At first, he was in and now he was out, and it made no sense because even though all this was going on, the connection kept getting stronger. Every time we would get together, it would usually turn into lovemaking, and every time it did, it only got better, and we became more creative and the experiences were all wonderful and unique. It was perplexing; none of it made any sense. I started to question everything. I could see how much this was affecting me now. It was starting to hurt, like an open wound.

I wanted to see him, and he kept telling me he couldn't see me.

I said, "Why not?"

"I'm too busy. I have my kids and I just don't have time," London said. These excuses and avoidance went on for a few days, and then turned into weeks.

I became very brazen one day and said, "Okay, well, let's just have a sex date then."

I remember that this got his attention and he said, "Okay, come on over."

I got to his house and made us drinks. He looked over at me with a smirk on his face. He said, "What are you wearing under that jacket?"

And I said, "Nothing."

He said, "I want to see."

I took off my jacket and he started to kiss me. He took me by my hand. With the jacket off, he didn't have to take the time to undress me. He didn't even take the time to take my heels off, either, so they stayed on. He looked me over and said, "Nice panties. You look very classy."

I laughed and said, "I'll take that compliment."

He put his hand to his mouth as to figure something out, and he said, "I want you to lean over."

And I said, "What?"

"I'm going to tell you how I want you," London said. He repeated himself and gave me further instructions.

He said, "Put one of your legs on the bed and balance yourself with your foot and lean over."

I was thinking this guy is such a control freak, but then I did it. He said, "You're going to feel me inside of you now…don't move."

I said, "Okay." And then I did.

London was inside of me and he was telling me not to move and I was finding this impossible. I wanted to move. I wondered, "Was he kidding?"

I wanted to feel this, too, to take it all in, but that was his point and he wanted to seduce me; he wanted to be the one to tell me when I could have pleasure.

He put his hands over my hips and started to thrust inside of me. He said, "I'm going to enjoy you right now, but I want you to be still."

I said, "Okay," but again, I was having a really hard time remaining still.

He was having fun with me and even more fun dominating this sexual encounter.

Then he shifted his attention a little and said, "Now I want you to see me inside of you right now. Come to the edge of the bed and watch me."

I did and he got on his knees and he took one of my legs and gracefully put it over his shoulder. Then he looked into my eyes and I saw that look again. He wasn't able to hide his feelings for me in the moment. His desire for me would overtake him and his eyes told me a different story.

He let me enjoy him and I got lost in his eyes, too. He knew (and knows) he has this power over me. It was almost like he could hypnotize me with his eyes. I felt like I could make love to just his eyes, metaphorically speaking.

He grabbed my face because he was overcome with pleasure and he said, "Are you ready to finish?"

And I said, "Yes," and he nodded in the affirmative and we found our orgasmic bliss,* together.

We got dressed and he walked me to the door. He put his hand up to give me a high five and I looked at his hand, and I looked back to his face. I was thinking, "Really? Really? *Really?*"

But, yes, he was really trying to "high-five" me and I glared at him, rolling my eyes.

He said to me, "You don't really conform to the rules of society, do you?" So many times with London, I just had no words. His words, I felt, were so disrespectful to me. I would rather just walk away than to argue with him.

---

* *Toes curling moment.*

101

But the impact his words had was so real, and it was always so hurtful to hear what I felt were coldhearted remarks. His words would cut me so deeply. Yet this pull would only get stronger as time came to pass.

"I Don't Do Labels"

To be on the Twin Flame Journey means that it is the time of looking in the mirror, like a double-edged sword that penetrates within. It is the energetic match of substance that attracts all the internal, to be shown on the external. This represents the initiations to victory of self. The energy of disintegration being shared between us, in synthesis, feels heavy and dense, but this is the rite of passage. The journey is about mastery and returning to our natural state, this being the archetype of the living light.

However, my energetic body is in turmoil. It feels like a struggle that begins from within, starting from the soul. It feels deep, like a labyrinth…a confusing feeling designed to keep me returning to this place deep inside of me. This energetic turbulence starts to unsettle my physical being and it feels like a stronghold; this is the most notable feeling. It is like the confusing structure of the labyrinth's design and it feels like discord. This feeling is reflected profoundly, but as much as this was on the inside, so too is it on the outside. The strong fondness the relationship has over me sends me into a period of floundering, fueled by an urgency of passion as alchemy is taking place. This process is changing matter by raising its resonance into a higher frequency…into pure energy, true love; however, the disturbance within that experience literally cracked open my heart by the magnitude of the energy exchange.

It is to presume that one knows not the soul, for the bestowed despondency was casting an awareness of the disheartened feeling and clarifying the shadows and the knowing of who we are: the yin and the yang. It is then that our alluring soul dance commences. The

103

adamant* heart is the resulting transmutation of the bodies of form that breathe his sympathy thereafter, rendering the effects of internal submission that take hold of my endearment to his reverence. There is an indictment of steadfast hasting,** a call to honor, marking the exalt of this dance on the realm of freedom, as we soar to novel curiosity. For this love is beyond the 3-D creation and beyond even the 4-D dimension of truth. It is an opposite with no opposite: No birth, no death, only alchemy or a transmutation of atomic and energetic oscillation, for it lives beyond the spheres. It is a spirit that was manifest in the Universe outside of self. Love itself is to experience the unseen and ponder what is seen, what is concrete, and what is abstract.

I want to hold such regard as the keen bond, enthralled by all that is and the sexuality and the rawest of titillation. The experience of creation, through the third energy of pureness, is matter solidified. Pure matter is felt of the most elevated sentimentality that I've ever bore, equating to the ferment of a blaze, yet tethered to rudiments of the regal, that of the watchful eye, by vision, that takes on the acquaintance to mind. What is it, then, to see, for the remnant of mind absorbs the sleuth of guile? This is the mystery of nature, for it is neither solely material nor entirely spiritual.

The intuitive mind is the root of the sacred gift in par with crude nature, the gist of lawlessness, for the element of sense is that there is no sense. There are no constraints when it comes to sexual nature; it is a stage of the reckless freedom. In the coming into the divine nature of sexuality, the walk is like being blindfolded and led, but there are no rules given, only the understanding of that, that it happened, and it would then be met with the consequence of emotion. It is trickery of the mind, for the mind feels all the elation, but the absence of the day's glimmer, as the night is the more construct naivety, and sincerity was the adversary. What was it to be in foe with nature, the celestial being of divine mind, for it is in the sagacity of shrewdness, as the comprehension of such glee, an astuteness of stride?

---

* Adamant: A legendary rock or mineral to which many, often contradictory, properties were attributed, formerly associated with diamond or lodestone.
** Hasting: Swiftness of motion; speed.

Yet, the path forward is blinding to my eyes, for the vision I saw in my mind's divination is that of discord when it is not in harmony with the spheres, for the pomposity of the moment gives the enticement of ineptness; the mind wants strategy over the duplicity of the smoke in the mirror.

It had been ordained, this soul dance. It is to know the harmony of the spheres, as the entire cosmos is all in the existence within them. This is the orbital resonance, like the words that flow, Venus and Mars…like the Goddess of Love with her God of War. It is in the meaning of the classic tempera Renaissance painting of sensual love where the pleasures of the mind at play disarms, as love unarmed conquers all. However, Venus and Mars continue their celestial dance in the orbit of the heavens for as long as their light shines below at the characters that are its mere reflection. A tantalizing dance would ensue with tidings of utterances from the air beyond, like a poem of expression, its aspiration for a declaration of sovereign acquaintance, the illumination of the odyssey's emergence. A complete eclipse of the heart transpires, for the seize herein, as the twilight hithers the sibyl of ancient divination. It is a bona fide moving of the air of heaven, the awakening of the four chambers, the cardinal guidance, the four elements, the regarded center of thought, the vital essence.

Embellishment of spire consumes the mind, the audacity of throne. The march of the step changes, for the drums sound in a flourish of heavenly storm and a call of the trumpet registers the spirit of secret prophecy. Dismay by the vision sent, for before the sight was the light of day, the infallible; it is yielded to the rites of love. It is a language that comes in time. It is a sacred love and with it, it carries beauty, but a truth to no avail.

As the key unlocks inherent wisdom, it is a formula of intrigue, but it is accompanied by a drama of impassioned dangers and the unearthing of tender wounds.* A eulogy of sagaciousness,** fairly

---

* Sybil: Prophetess; fortune teller.
** Sagaciousness: The mental ability to understand and discriminate between relations (discernment, judgement)

an alliance of intuition, but with skewed disposition, for a strong mind and a fragile heart is the relic. It is in the heart that lives the consummated dilemma of the impasse of love and death. Here in the quantum reality, there is duality, math, and the mirror symmetry of reflection. The exact denotation of alliance and true nature of the ordained matters of the heart-integrated system, a timorous confession of treason, that of mind to heart, and the utterance of the despondency of time. As perception is the inaptness of sequence, pretentious thoughts of feats and poise are lost, a ruling and consuming passion of the heart transfigures to the reigning, prevailing force.

Scene XIV

Early in the day London called and told me he'd like to go out on a date with me. I thought: "Really."

It had been a while since our last "date" and needless to say, I was excited. I told him I would work on arranging a sitter, and then we could meet up.

He texted me later, cancelling the date out of nowhere. I was upset because I was already ready, and I was looking forward to spending time with him.

He said, "It's too late. I've already made dinner for myself."

I said, "Well, let me come over then." He said that was fine and to come on over.

I showed up at his house and again, he was in one of his moods. It was strange how London would go from being 100 percent in the moment and present when we were intimate to arguing with me out of nowhere. It seemed like I couldn't keep up with the highs and lows of his disposition or this relationship.

We sat down in his living room and he said, "It seems like you want to talk."

"London, I do."

I continued, "I want to know why you're so mean to me; why don't you treat me like a lady?"

I'll never forget the words he said to me and the exact expression on his face when he said them. He looked me squarely in the eyes and said, "Do you think I'm going to treat you any differently because of your gender?"

I was processing his words, but I wanted to scream at him and say, "Of course, of course, I think you're going to treat me differently because I'm a lady!"

But the fact was that he didn't see this. His perspective hit a part of my mind that made me realize what type of "different" I was dealing with. His logic was logic, but it seemingly was on a very inhumane level.

His way of thinking was concrete and cemented by a different level of logic. He didn't have room for any outside influence to change his ideas. He was all about his thought process and there was no room for outside opposition to influence who he was; he stood behind his viewpoint, unwavering.

I was starting to feel like I had had enough of his B.S., both in person and by text. I said, "Do you want to just end this, London?"

He said, "If that's what you want."

I said, "You know what I want, but you're not going to give me what I want, so what's the point?"

"You don't even know what you want," he said.

"Of course I do."

"Then, tell me what it is that you want," said London.

I said, "I want you. I would like a relationship with you. I'd like to spend more time with you, and I'd like you to be the way you were with me when we first met. I'd like you to be my boyfriend."

He said, "I don't do labels."

I said, "Really? Why not?'

He said, "I've found when you put labels on things, they deteriorate very quickly afterward."

"What is it you're looking for, London, because that's what's so confusing," I said.

London didn't open up very often to me, but on this day, he did.

He said, "I want someone to love me the way my Mom and Dad loved each other."

He continued: "My Dad loved my Mom in a way I admired." He told me a story of when his father died, the year prior. His Dad had left his mother money in cash that he had never told her about. The point was that his father wanted to make sure his mother was taken care of, and that was what love meant to them. He said, "Yes, they had their issues, but they stood behind one another no matter what, and that's what counts."

London almost started crying when he told me this story. He was looking away, looking into space, looking into his mind of memories of his parents when they were together.

I wanted to go over to him. I wanted to hug him, but I noticed his expression had changed. He started to reflect on when his father was dying and the suffering it caused him. I could see London's pain and anger. I was trying to be a good listener, and I wanted to be more to London in that moment, but he wouldn't allow it.

Then he said, "I think you need to leave now."

I could see he wasn't in a good space and respecting this, I said good night, turned on my heel, and left.

This was the first and only time London ever let me see his vulnerable side. This moment would allow me to see a glimpse of his psyche as it related to his early life. I began to understand him from this moment in a different way, seeing his childhood wounding, which reflected my own unhealed wounds.

Cruel Intent

The Gnosis,* like a messenger with a letter of science, gives rise to the inner light as the mid-Heaven reveals its insight of the true nature of our being of the Divine Masculine and Divine Feminine polarities. The philosophy (Prophecy) of the Twin Flame dynamic is based on the polarity of everything and nothing, as everything in your life changes the dynamic of it all. For in its wake, the seal is placed over us like an experience of our life's virtue, witnessed through the eyes of love, for this alone changes life itself.

The awakening to the higher love takes hold and here, too, is where the soul weeps and vows to find love as the nature of this love is to fight for reason, as the heart sets forth the journey. The bones, flesh, and heart follow like a spell that understands no other than the person that has cast it. For the solider within stands tall and above all else, it's like the Warrior Goddess archetype, a soldier of ransom who seeks answers of pure heart. Nothing will stand in her way, nor will stop the conquest before the dragon nature within…holding the intent to slay anything in its path. Like a quick, fire-breathing weapon to extract evil, down to the very bottom of the soul. The heart sees truth, in black or white, and feels the constant tug of the spirit to find the heart's mercy, for the conquest to bear is the muse of personified love.

The inflaming wrath of the soul takes hold, for one understands this polarity of everything as a creative chariot that spins out of Heaven and is given to us with care. This vessel is tamed by the tempered

---

* *Gnosis: It is best known from Gnosticism, where it signifies a knowledge or insight into humanity's real nature as divine, leading to the deliverance of the divine spark within humanity from the constraints of earthly existence.*

nature of within and responds to the voice of the heart and "The Heavens."

The life cycle is connected with the Sun as this represents "Fire" and the rising of light, for with each day is the promise of a new beginning. But the flame is fire and fire produces heat, and the nature of the Twins is the passion that exists in the connection. This same flame is carried by our hearts, with the inspiration for new creation and the ability to rise again in new life and vitality.

Through the Fall from the high heavens, the love remains with us, and is experienced instantly. And the separation from this love feels the same, just pure love. The deep wound is left like a gaping hole, for the spirit is like a ransom with no avail, the mist, the brink of despair, the sick soldier, the wounded warrior, the cusp of a love that finds no distance and no true duty but the uttermost power over the soul.

This is where in the mind of all minds, one learns the verdict of the "Fall." It means to climb to the heights of the highest of high love and then to free-fall, bloodied and burned by the flame and sword of true love. The insight of the "deep wound" leaves its scar to bear, for the soul's poor heart is left with a freeze of cold that finds no comfort in the temperance of night.

Heaven's wrath is experienced, but the blessing of our true nature is felt within your blood, a thousand seeds of electrified current running deep throughout. There exists a knowing of a home within and the feeling of melancholy, for our soul knows only oneness, pure energy, untainted love. The gates of the heavens are opened, and wisdom is bestowed, as the heart is opened to true love's utter power.

This love takes one back to the start, to the zero point of destruction, but it is also the point of creation. The start of "Life" from the very beginning.

What is life, from the tempest of flow, the connection from birth, the embryo of time? The Eternal Spirit with grace UNITED the

Twins, in the unity of God. So shall it be and so it is, the supreme secret of all ancient initiations. He has fortified the connection of this symmetrical entity to bind the pattern of beauty, like the Rose. The bond is that of death, of life, and of rebirth and the eternal bond of wholeness.

The majesty of the bond holds this beauty, for within it lies the force of supreme power. This love would set us free but imprison us to it at the same time. The mysticism of plea surrounds its light and the beam that is placed directly over the heart is set forth to the unlocking of the Holy Grail.

The journey unveils its beauty as the flow of life, like wisdom that cascades the living water and flows like a river. It is a flow that resides within that awakens to the spirit without. This would be the lesson of detachment, for we would need to understand the love inside of us before we could understand the love that existed outside of us.

This union is when two bodies merge into oneness and the experience of the Kundalini snake rises from within. The serpent awakens the third eye, down to the very root, and here you feel true love. The divine energy located herein is energetically activated and releases. The rising up occurs through the energy centers of the spine. When awakened, the emotions felt are inundated by the emotional body, tempering the spiritual and physical connection. For when Twins are brought forth again, the understanding of the experience coincides with the explosive nature of life force energy and thus the endurance of its extreme highs and lows.

This bridge between the opposites, the charged polarity of divine nature, joins us together in cosmic bliss, as the energy cascades into fermented wine.

Scene XV

London continued to test my patience. I texted him and he had become completely indifferent with me. This is how it was with him. One day would be amazing and the next would be the exact opposite. I was thinking very seriously about just breaking things off, because my mind couldn't stand what he was doing to me. I felt the emotional instability he was creating in my life was just too difficult. I needed honesty from him.

At this point, his love hurt, and it was cruel, heartless, and painful. My heart needed answers. He was leaving for New Zealand soon and he'd be gone for 22 days. This became his new favorite excuse to not see me, although he kept our affair going by text. But on this day, I needed clarification.

We decided to meet, and I got ready. I was feeling good about seeing him, until I did. When I looked at him, one word came to mind: "Ugly," (not in the physical sense, but in an emotional sense). "Ugly" is all I can see written across his face. I was beginning to think that London had an unresolved mental health issue, like post-traumatic stress disorder, because his moods, frankly, scared me.

He let me in, with hardly a greeting, and said very rudely: "I don't have a lot of time."

I didn't even know how to respond to the comment, so I took a seat at the table and watched as London came around to face me. He was direct and as he looked at me, he said, "I think I attract 'crazy.'"

I looked at him like, "Are you kidding?"

I was thinking in my head that he really wouldn't say this to my face, but that was exactly what he was doing. I was taken aback, but by this time, I was used to the shocking truths he shared with me, but not to say it made the blows any easier or less painful.

I stood up from my seat and looked him straight in the eye. "Do you think I'm crazy?"

He said, "Well, not **crazy**, like I'm going to need to arrest you and put you on a 51/50-hold-crazy, but *crazy*."

My eyes grew big and I glared at him. I let his words sit in my mind. The words registered in a space my mind had never visited before and this new place relayed a message of treachery.

I'll never forget the feeling that this statement impaled into my whole being. It was the wickedness of how someone's words could affect you in a way that was unspoken and cruel.

He started to speak without looking at me because my eyes were eating into his skull. He wasn't sure how to take this and his mind started wandering. He started speaking what was on his mind openly as if he were talking to a friend about a third person. He said, "Yes, crazy, like my first wife and like my second wife, crazy."

My mouth literally fell open, but no words were coming out. I watched him, and his cruel intent was settling in and had hit a spot in my heart that was very unnerving. He started reflecting, like he had just made up his mind about this. He looked at me in that moment and said, "Maybe it's something about me. Maybe I attract 'crazy.'"

He looked at me as if I was his friend and he was seeking advice. I was so beyond myself at this moment and my mind had many words for him. My mind wanted my voice to find these words, but my voice couldn't find the words because my heart was crushed by the insult. My mind was trying to not let my heart be overcome. My mind was trying to stay in control, but every bit of who I am was shaken. I was trying to focus, because I wanted my words to resound in this man's head, but first, my words needed to find my voice and they finally did.

I found his eyes and I made sure I had his attention. He had crossed a line with me.

I spoke very slowly and directly. I said, "Listen, it's not the type of women you attract. It is you! It's what you do to women that drives them crazy! It's your words. It's what you say and the way you say it. It's your mixed messages. It's your backward remarks. It's the way you make a woman feel that drives her crazy. It's you! It's what you do to the women. It's not the women, but you, who drives them crazy. It's your actions. They don't match your words, and this alone drives a woman crazy."

He stopped to interrupt me, and said very matter-of-factly, "No, that's not it."

I said, "I'm still talking." I continued very slowly. I wouldn't let him cut me off because my words needed to find him. I said, "Let me be specific with you so you can understand what I'm saying to you, just like when you say, 'You can see yourself in a relationship with me, but in the same breath, you say you can't.' Just like when you say, 'I don't want a girlfriend. I just want to have fun,' but you'll lead me on at the same time with 'Let's see where this goes.' Mixed messages! This kind of stuff will drive anyone crazy, especially women!"

He was giving me his "cop look," like, "Are you done?"

I could see that he had enough of what I had to say, but no, I wasn't done.

I went on to say, "What's bothering you is that you're not liking the fact that I can identify things about your character, your flaws, and clearly point them out to you."

He didn't like being called out on his flaws and he didn't like anyone to question him or his authority, much less make him reflect on how offensive he was. He didn't like his faults being put out in front of him and all his lies exposed in his face. No, he didn't like this!

I offended him and he was angry. I could see the expression change on his face. He looked at me like, "Oh, you want a challenge?" He smirked and said, "That's not true."

London is a quick thinker and he twists things around. He turned this on me and said, "You know something? You can't even say what you have to say. You hide behind your texts."

I looked up at him and started looking away, because frankly, I was scared. I knew his attack was coming back on me and now it was his turn; he had been patiently waiting.

He had a look in his eyes, and he knew it was his turn to speak. He said, "Yeah, that's right," while he nodded his head. "You know what I'm saying to you. You write all this stuff to me by text, but you can never say it to my face."

I looked at him for clarification because I wasn't sure exactly what he was referring to. Knowing he had my attention, he continued, "You know exactly what I mean. And you want to know something else?"

"What?" I said.

He said, "I would respect you a lot more if you would just say what you have to say and if you would stand up for yourself, but that's your problem…you can't!"

I said, "That's not true! I can, but I'm not as callous as you and I'm careful with my words."

I said to him, "You know, most girls would have told you to fuck off a long time ago…"

He stopped me at that and said simply, "Then be like most girls and tell me!"

I realized at that moment what he was saying to me and he was right. I couldn't tell him to his face to go fuck himself. I just didn't have it in me to be that way.

Our conversation was over. I couldn't listen to his cruel intent anymore, so I left, and I heard the door slam behind me as I walked out of his house. His insult had penetrated my brain and these injuries were fresh on my heart.

Mind Craft: Superhuman Abilities

To live is to question everything; it is to be a student of this love. This muse that one creates…the majesty of the curse of love lives amidst the chaos of life and in the "trying-to-figure-it-out" stages of inconsistencies. The emotions of love stray the sight and impoverish the body. The feeling of inadequacy is the clamor of these emotions, for they are too difficult to suppress. Amidst the reflection, sharpness of the sword prays the mind to bring the scent of blood to the heaviness of pain that is being experienced by the heart.

There is nowhere left to go, only to the hermit state of the soul, as we retreat in temperance. It is to go to this place, and here is this dwelling that one will find the truth of venom; it is the place of within, and it means to depart from everything without. A thousand fixed stars bequeath the meaning to it all. It is in the stars, the cosmic light of time, where one can reflect on the heart as the ego mind is dismissed and all else is revealed. This is the state of transcendence, the evermore, the state where you can get to the bigger picture of the soul. It is to transcend beyond the limits of the mind as it is to radiate on the frequency of the universe. Here the dichotomy of opposites merges, the darkness and light. It is the attraction that blinds the mind. The feeling, the vitality…here at this juncture…steams the addictive need, the positive and negative magnetism is a lure of the mind, like a compulsion for a substance, the crux of the soul.

What does it mean, however, as the emotional body washes over these complexities and the intricacies of the crux and the twists and turns become a reflection on the outside? For it is not the intellect that finds logic, but instead it is found by the unpretentious need of sincere want, the desire of the heart, that takes command of obscurities. It is

117

the subtleties of unconditional love, the path of the heart. The feeling is inexplicable, like a numbness or a contrived impulse, at the same time. It is a muse and a repellent, it is the integration of the other, it is the third energy formula, that chemical balance of pure lust and longing, and a consummation of the entire being. One must wonder if the integration is the formula or the person, or the connection, for the intellect is not a part of this equation.

It is the duplicity of the lunar cycle, the beginning of the end, the end of the beginning, for the perspective of all the elements reaches into the beyond to understand what it is that the skies of the heavens have poured over us. It is to understand the suit of cup of the divine, for it is not a substance of just gleam, but that of the element of the sun in vibrancy, the pureness of the realness of what is. The fire element is what gives it the most esteem.

We trudge forward, and our magnetic pull always brought us back to each other. As in time, it is the call of the eagle, the dance, if you will, to understanding this concept from a bird's-eye view. It is to meet in flight and crash, while in full force with no concept of the bearing, as the power of the ruble and the fall to the death, in which lay the secrets to this ritual. It is a ritual of symbolic death of the ego and it will be made to do, over and over and over again, until the formula becomes prime.

The dormant codes of the DNA structure of our genetic makeup wakes up. Like the rapture of the heart, its desire is to understand more fully the Twin in the physical world. As one awakens to the subconscious mind, it gives rise to the remembering, and our truth mocks our being. The secrets that hide in the Twin Flames are that we share the same soul (light) and blueprint structure. One's heart holds the mystical knowledge of our Twin Flame connection and the heart links one to their soul's connection. Mystery becomes unveiled through the inner light luminance as we become the masters of the light, and it is a bond beyond death. It is the connection to the thread (the etheric cord) that connects us to the spiritual world. It is what gives "LIFE," as the heart is known to carry with it truth and justice for the afterlife. Our heart's intelligence is the common core and strongest link to our Twin.

To seek to understand becomes the process to no avail, for we must experience the past to seek illumination from the Akashic records, the keeper of time, to gain further insight into our souls' journey.

Created together as "ONE," we come into existence, connected by the etheric cord. In the same way that "death" and "birth" are each other's Twin, as one, we hold this same polarity within. As Twins, one is not without the other. This is the intimate link and identical true mirror of self. Like all things created in set order, First and Last, like the Uroboros* that is symbolic of wholeness and infinity.

Through the process of purification the Twin Flames undergo, our hearts become pure again and only in this form can we connect to our spirit body (higher self).

In the beginning, thought was spoken to word, and "Let there be light" aligned with love; this is the magic of co-creation and making our thoughts our reality.

The opposite of light (birth) is darkness (death) or the transition of the Sun cycle to the moon cycle or day to night. All things have their natural cycle and with a beginning comes an end, to have anew.

Scene XVI

I was working at my store and London stopped by and asked me if I wanted to have lunch. Today he had a stoic disposition. Since our last conversation, he had been very elusive, but today, he seemed like he wanted to talk. He was hiding behind his ego and I could still tell that he was scared of emotion because he doesn't offer me any clue what feelings reside inside.

---

*   *Uroboros: A circular symbol depicting a snake, or less commonly a dragon, swallowing its tail, as an emblem of wholeness or infinity.*

We walked, but I struggled from within to leave our troubles and disagreements behind us. I carried them here in the present, as I couldn't contain the nature of ambiguity that these worries carry, and so we walked with the burdens. Our conversation was unsettling. I struggled to hold back everything that was inside, as it would only add fuel to the fire.

It seemed that London couldn't deal with any kind of emotion. Even an inkling of the trials that were testing us would send him running and then I wouldn't hear from him for days. But now every part of this connection only seemed to push him away from me. We were holding on by a thread, but I didn't understand at the time that it was our thread of redemption.

I couldn't hold back, though. I had to put it out there. I said, "London, you give me so little of your time. I just want to know what changed?"

Judging from his reaction, I knew I had crossed the line, for even an utterance or suggestion of anything that remotely touched on feelings was taboo with him. To overstep my boundary with him meant he would hold back even more on our connection, which was shared with me through the gift of his time. He had already told me, at this point, that things were not of a serious nature between us. To talk to London about feelings was virtually to open the doors to the threshold of the dawn, for this was where the shadows resided...this ghost, so to speak, that London carried. To me, it was all of the unknowns.

To tell him what was going on around me meant he would think I was crazier than he already thought I was. To tell him how offensive and cruel he was, that was to open the door to animosity. He verbalized his conviction when I asked him the question: "Are you purposely trying to push me away? Because you're doing a good job."

I understood where this statement put us, with him not wanting what I wanted, so in retrospect, it was going to push him away further. But all I wanted was to get closer to him and develop a friendship. I really didn't want to bring about any more hindrances; I felt powerless. I refrained from saying anything more. Adversity to us was the sanction of my truth. The only thing I really wanted was to be with him and to be in his presence, the paradox of it all.

So, we walked, and I let it go. He quickly changed the subject and I just went with it. He was telling me about his day and then he turned and asked me about my day. I wanted so badly to hold back everything…but my heart didn't know how. Whenever I looked into his eyes, I just melted and all I wanted to do was hug him and tell him how I felt about him, not about mundane happenings, but about him and me. As it was with London, he wouldn't let me tell him. When he saw the effect he had on me, he turned away.

We reached our destination and we went inside and ate. I had a salmon dish, because I wasn't very hungry. I ordered a drink because I knew I needed it today to settle my mind about this love. Being in his presence was very difficult for me because it just cemented to me how deeply my affection for him was. I let the alcohol drown my inhibitions and sadness instead and I put on a smile to mask my true emotions. I remember that I could barely eat my food and I offered it to him instead. He consumed the remnants of my love for him, as I watched.

We finished and walked outside. I couldn't hold my emotions in any longer and I felt like this was coming to an end, so I blurted out, "Why don't you let me talk to you about my feelings?"

London grabbed me and he pushed me up against a pole. I was caught off guard and shocked by this impulsive act. I looked him in the eyes. He possessed a stoic calm that commanded my attention.

He said, "This is not what you think it is."

I said, "What?"

"This is something else. You don't see that?" London said.

He was looking at me in the eyes. He had me cornered and he looked deeper into my eyes to see if I had an answer for him, but I really

121

didn't get it. I had some kind of knowing of what he was saying and asking me, but I really didn't know specifically what it was or how to articulate it, as he was still extracting and dissecting my answer from my eyes.

He released his grip on me and gave me a cast of light from his stare, as he released this intellect to my cognizance. I couldn't look away from him as my mindfulness took me to the allure of the paranormal.

I felt this twitch in my mind, like mind-craft, knowledge above and beyond human understanding. It was like someone had turned on a switch to superhuman abilities. I knew what he was saying to me, not with full understanding, but with foresight that this moment was for him to divulge to me his hindrance to affection, for he understood this notion before I did. However, my mind was only becoming introduced to what he was saying.

I wasn't going to let this topic, this struggle to understand, go, so we picked this conversation up by text.

"Yes, you're right, London. I couldn't tell you to your face what I wanted to say, but I will say what I have to say to you because I need you to know how I feel. At this point, your love is painful. I have to let this out and you're not going to stop me. London, listen, I don't know what I did to you to deserve to be treated this way.

He wrote back: "I see too many red flags."

I responded, "You see too many red flags? No, these are not red flags you see! This is just you seeing me responding to all the mixed messages you give me. One day, it's this, and the next day, it's the exact opposite. Your actions DON'T match your words."

I was getting furious with him because he was being very direct and telling me I was crazy. I replied, "I'm ready to tell you what I need to say and that is that you're cold-hearted. If you don't want to continue to see me, then let's say it's done and both call it that."

We didn't talk for a few days, but I was so distraught over him and over this. I sent him a text after a few more days had passed, and I said, "London, I'm sorry."

He sent a response, asking me to come by and see him for coffee. "I'm not ready to throw in the towel," he said.

The Spiritual Cross

The understanding of polarity rises to the surface of consideration. It is the advantage of the eye to see from the depths of the soul, believing in the guidance of the third eye for the accuracy of the bearing, the nature of creation, and the connection to it all. It is to seek the truth above all, the sworn truth to the other, the duality of conception, the core of the being when it is no more. Fairly a note of measure, the cord of the heart, the pitter, the patter, the sound, and the run. Indeed, to see in the darkest of mirage the gales of grace, the eternal candle, as once it was only the sound, that of love and laughter of the heart, to know the divine, to be one in this light. It is without the tangles over the eyes, the grief of heart to only feel the joy. In the pitiness, the flounder of ordinance, that have the sight of love. Sorrowful emotion, the enemy of the mistress, and the spirit will only find luminescence of desire, lust in the passing. Who might call this pity, for it is the pity of sorrow to know that love is the darkest of emotions and the lightest favor, exulted in strife, for the markings are written on the walls of perfect love?

Is it foolish to fall in love, as the wind sweeps you off your feet and only the gold tincture of understanding stands alone, for the unsteady feet bear the verge of conduit…on the brink of connection…for the virtuous nature of languishing? The simile of adoration, the tenders of innocence; for the novice it was the seamstress' needle, the sobering of the soul's unease. For the search of the soul's retrieval is to quilt together the fragmented soul.

This warrants the mind, and the bearing of false witness to no man, for the scribe is written, the knight with his armor will come, the flesh will knock on the door of descent, for here is where one finds the strength in all the lineage of time stirring the call, abiding to the soul. Here the soul finds its voice, for no other is stronger than the pulsating heart, the obedient, submissive nature of action for the devotion to the disposition of sounds that manifest from the heart's calls, the desires, the fire, the flame, the spark, the worship of thought. There is no other sound but silence.

Knock, I say, for the chambers tremble, and the voice finds its words, like hissing snakes, as they twist and dissipate into the vision. The "Aha" moment of the kiss, as the tongue strikes the other and the violence of the attack turns to passion, a proposal of heart, a prologue to the intense provoking of good versus evil. A confession to truth in the eye of the all-knowing, reverent love in the end, and the beginning the link of your pain, the link of your pleasure, your link to the eternal flame of fire. By the imposed rhetorical knowing, I am a prisoner to the God of love, for he would sway me, bemuse me, sing to me, entice me, and humble me all at the same time. Will was released, for divine will was the holder of soul journey, as the knave of whichever suit I wore would reflect tomorrow's tone. As one's acquaintance grew to the knowing, ominous was the hour, as the hour of today strikes the same sound as the hour of tomorrow, for it is to look beyond sight alone and trust the God of love instead, the holder of the eternal flame.

Scene XVII

London stopped by my shop again out of the blue. I was happy to see him, delighted, actually, and we began kissing intensely. We were in the moment of a passionate kiss and then all of a sudden, he abruptly pulled away and said he had to leave. I wondered what had happened. Not wanting to make it even more awkward with words, I said, "Okay, well, I guess we'll talk later."

I went to hug him and say goodbye, and I'll never forget what he did. He looked at me as if I were a foreign creature and backed up, all the way to the wall. I took a step forward, and he was cornered, with nowhere to go. I was looking at him, confused, and then I took another step toward him and he made a cross with his hands, and put it toward me. The second he did this, I backed off and then he circled around me with his hands in a cross, held up high, until he was able to get out of my space. He never turned his back to me; he just left the store without saying anything. I was just watching him. It was if the whole scene played out in slow motion in front of me, with him leaving me a message in his departure of epoch* and then, he was gone.

This man brought me to the threshold of contemplation. London was so complex, so complicated and the relationship with him was completely bewildering. I wanted so badly to figure it all out, but the cross, it was an innuendo that left an intimate feeling of an association to spiritual connotation.

I remember feeling puzzled, as the conceptual aspect of my thought considered this act. Why on Earth would London hold up a cross to me? It was the most unusual thing anyone had ever done to me.

Although London tried so hard to separate his feelings, I found he was having a hard time doing so as one thing we both understood is that our connection was very strong, even though we wanted to end it all. This connection felt like an innate desire for the other. When we were with each other, it would manifest into a very intense moment. It was passion, a force of attraction, a fire felt from deep within, but an attraction that was misunderstood on the outside.

He wanted to meet up again and he called me the same night. I thought London probably wanted to settle things with us and I agreed, as I had a very unsettled feeling about us, so I told him, yes, we could meet up.

We decided to go downtown again to our usual spot and have a few drinks. We ordered our usual cocktails and we quickly became intoxicated. He asked if I wanted to go back to my store to sober up. We barely made it past closing my shop's door and we were both

---

* Epoch: A period of time in history or a person's life, typically one marked by notable events or particular characteristics.

pulling each other's clothes off. We made it back to the black curtain and we stopped for a minute. I looked over at him and as I was about to pull the curtain, he said, "No, don't close it."

At the time, I was a little reluctant, but instantly, his words spoke to me and I understood why he said this, because we didn't need to shield our love from the world. Our love felt so pure and genuine. It was like a natural, open-pouring source of water, like rain falling from heaven above. I was very much in the moment and this love would overflow with the desire I had for him. It really didn't make a difference to me, either, where we were or who saw us.

He pulled my black stool out and sat on it, and then pulled me to him. He couldn't take the passion, though, so he picked me up, taking me into his arms. We started to kiss. Then he took my legs and wrapped them around him, and he walked me up the stairs. He stopped at the top of the stairs and said, "Here, this is where I want you."

He pulled off the rest of my clothes and he was looking at my body. I was about to turn off the light, and London said, "No! I want you to remember me in this moment, and plus, I want to see you."

He was wearing jeans and started to take them off, letting me watch him. He pulled off his undershirt and he came down and started to kiss my neck. I could smell his sweat and I could feel the wetness of it as his face was pressed up against mine. I could see his yearning for me when I would open my eyes, but this was mostly sensed in the way I could sense his hunger for my body.

He removed his underwear, grabbing me by my arms. He turned me around and started to kiss me on the back of my neck. Pinning my body under his, he started to get a little assertive and he pulled my legs apart and I felt his warmth. This feeling was like nothing else I've ever experienced. I let my head fall back onto his chest and welcomed the trance we were going into. We were finding each other on a different plane...our souls had come together and that was the appetite we felt to find each other this way.

His knees started to bother him, and he told me he had to stand up. He stood up, and I felt him reach down to me. He pulled me up by my arms, but he didn't want me to stand up fully, so he brought me to my knees; he was in my face. When I close my eyes now, remembering and writing about this, I can see London as if he were really here, his manliness in my face, the shape, the size. Desire is the best word I have for him in this moment, as I am forced to re-live our story out on paper within the pages of this book.

The beauty of his manly body inundates my mind, for he embodied my body and all of its senses along with articulated desire in the flesh. When he was about to climax, he grabbed my hair in his hands. He said, "Hey…"

I looked up at him, and he asked if he could release his passion in my mouth. I was wondering why he was even asking, but I answered and said, "yes." He did and I tasted him in my mouth. He looked at me and said, "Bitter?" And I said, "yes." The taste of him penetrated my taste buds and my memory recorded this as the palatable indulgence of the natural, liquified affinity for my London.

It's difficult to articulate the way I felt about this man because I had never felt this way before and I didn't quite understand it myself. London was the most heightened sensual being I had ever encountered. It was as if he was made exactly the way my senses desired a man. If my mind could compare him to anything and who he was to my soul as a way to disclose understanding of this experience, it would be like the desire that one feels for food.

I'll describe it this way. Imagine you are on the vacation of a lifetime, somewhere absolutely beautiful. Everything is perfect, the weather is amazing and tropical, the company with you is your dream lover, the scenery is surreal, and you are having the most perfect, most incredible romantic dinner. The food is delicious, and you're taking everything in for the beauty of it all, and you know you are ready for dessert.

The waiter comes around and in his beautiful foreign accent, describes what is on the dessert menu and you don't even let him get past the first choice, saying, "Yes, bring me that!" He comes back with the most extraordinary looking desert you have ever laid your eyes on, and your mind is thinking that the waiter's words, with the beautiful accent and all of the charm, didn't do this dessert any kind of justice, but then the experience only keeps getting better.

You already knew the dessert was going to be exquisite, but it isn't until you put your fork into it and take that perfect piece and put it in your mouth, that you know. Your eyes get big, your senses are heightened with the pleasure, you emit a sound from your mouth, something along the lines of "Mmmmmmm," and your eyes glaze over. It feels like heaven, this combination of flavors coming together. Your mouth is literally making love to the taste. The pleasure is felt not only by your mouth, but it registers in your brain, too, as something amazing. This decadent dessert is someone's art, someone's perfect creation of sweet, elegant flavors. The texture is perfect, the taste is out-of-this-world good, and it's like nothing you have ever consumed before. It melts in your mouth, you close your eyes and enjoy the moment and then when it is finished, and all you want to do is to take another bite. You are left with longing. You want more. You want to relive the experience. You want to taste it again. You want that heightened pleasure. You want that perfect package of self-indulgence.

That was London to me; he was my human indulgence of personified pleasure. He was God's art to my soul. My soul craved this man like the sweet pleasure that he literally was to me. My body wanted him for the sensual beauty of who he was, and my heart wanted him because he melted every part of it. As for my mind, it just couldn't get enough of the high that London made me feel.

When the moment was over, London held my face in his hands. I looked up at him and said, "You're not circumcised." He looked at me with his cop expression and said, "You just noticed?" I said, "Yes, I kind of just noticed."

Just like our love, in the moment, it was very difficult to recognize things, but as I look back, it was what our love was: a natural love... uncircumcised and pure.

London's Double-Edged Sword

Our love became such a conflicting mix of emotions, the aftermath of all of it was cruel. I questioned how something that felt so incredibly perfect could feel so petrifying at the same time. The highs were incredible and undeniable, but the other side of this relationship was now revealed as our masks came off. This is when our true colors shone through us and our reflections were revealed through the other. I was able to read this man through his very soul as I searched his eyes, and he was able to do the same. This process is impenetrable, as words became our weapons. Emotions were dismissed because truth was the only fortress that was unearthed. Truth held and unfolded our realities, as seen through a glass of light that resounded with the shifting of energy where good could not enter this space until the bad was removed and addressed.

London had this ability over me, and I possessed it over him because we were Twins from the same energy source. There exists a supernatural power that resides in this space. One can use this power in both ways, but when used in a distorted manner, it could be vicious and cruel.

London would often stab me with his words. With his comments, he would dig deep and cut me open and then twist the blade and watch me bleed. He would put his sword in the most hurtful spot in my soul and hold it there and would not allow me to move. I was pinned under his words of candor to me as I was made to look at my truth and I couldn't run from it. I was made to stare at it in the face and take the pain that was concealed.

The pain so deep that only a sword could get to it, and London had this sword. The sword was specially crafted; it was double-edged and sharp, and his ability to use it was like that of a skilled swordsman. Its depth was so profound that only the stronghold of the power of his words could find it. I was literally pinned up against a cold surface, and there was no remorse in this space. There was no fighting back, there was nowhere to turn to, and there was no turning around or going back. There was no left or right, there was no black or white, only truth. Words that carried so much power...my truth was spit at me in my face, while I was being stabbed with the meaning of my certitude.

One might wonder why I endured it all and what kept me coming back to this insanity. The fact was, it was the connection. London and I connected in a different way, we connected on a different space and in a different sphere; this connection was on a soul level. It was felt in many planes, but most strongly in the sexuality of the union and in this space, it felt like a high, a high that was addictive. It was the strongest high I knew, and the addiction was something I had no self-control over. This man was able to take me to this place and so London became an addiction to me.

With all the chaos I had going on in my life, I needed London as my distraction. He kept me sane during these trying days, but I didn't realize how dangerous this would become. Just like anything that is pure, from the purest source, it was toxic. But at the time, my simple mind did not comprehend this plane we would get to, the fourth dimension. At this time there were too many other things that fogged up my mind to allow me to understand this and what it was. It felt like a fantasy. That was the way my mind processed it, but this fantasy went beyond my wildest dreams. The allure, the seduction, the pleasure, the illusion of it all. I just had to call him and tell him I needed a distraction and he knew exactly how to give me that. He took my mind off my problems. He took me to a place in my mind where I had never been. We were beginning to feel this place together. It was unknown to us, and we sensed that it was something different and that we would reach it from this union. But that became our riddle, because the more of him I got, the more attached to him I became. The more attached I became, the more I needed him. The more I needed him, the more entangled we became until we were intertwined. But I couldn't have him, not the way I wanted him, or the way my mind comprehended at the time that I wanted him. That was the problem as our relationship was meant to unfold here on the earthly realm, but for the purpose of enlightenment and *not* the purpose of a relationship. This created conflict within us, and no understanding was rendered to us at the time because it is not the natural course we knew and understood about relationships.

These forces, like magnets, that brought us together were (and are) too strong, and our relationship constantly seemed to intensify. But that intensity worked both ways. Not only did the intimacy get better every time because that was very much at the forefront of the relationship, but the arguments and the pain would take a new manifestation. The sex felt like the best sexual experience of my life times 100. All our senses were heightened during the act. But so was the fighting and the lows felt by the experience of this union. Most of the conflict started from things that were very insignificant; however, they would blow up and get to a place where there was no way to take back control.

This affiliation of two souls was conflicting on so many levels, and the union was a complete paradox of emotions. The one thing that was understood between us was that when we were together, all our problems would fall away. I would literally lose myself in him, and I saw this reflect through him in the same way. The other understanding I had was that everything changed the very moment that I met London: Every problem fell away, every thought changed, every part of my body transformed.

My soul recognized who he was. He had come into my life to change me, not in a simple-minded way, but in the most extreme way a person could possibly change. The transformation would come from the inside. It started with my mind, then my heart, then my spirit, and finally, my soul. He linked to me as if he rewrote my DNA the minute he stepped into my life. Every molecule inside of me was changed with a renewed coding and my identity changed with it. He was not just a person who came into my life, but a soul who found a home with me and through me. Our connection was that of our energy source coming together. The moment we met, this energy was rewired by a volt of the spiritual light that was bestowed upon us. But with the light also comes darkness and there were a lot of shadows being cast as we embarked upon territory that was uncharted and unfamiliar to us.

Scene XVIII

London and I began to have a very distinct moment of distance. He was not being obvious about it to the point where he verbalized it (after some time of not seeing me). I didn't understand it because whenever we were in the moment, he couldn't deny how he felt about me. That was why I always felt like I had to see him. I felt like if I could just see him and make love with him, then everything would be okay. I knew that when we were together, we would find that blissful place and everything else would fall away. This is the connection we had with each other; I know he felt this same way. He couldn't deny me how he felt in each of those moments. I could see it in his eyes; it was like nothing else mattered when we were together.

The day was special, and I remember it so clearly. I was getting ready. As usual, I was thinking about him and I knew in my heart that I would see him on this day. I called and I didn't really give London a choice. I told him I was going to bring coffee over and that I just wanted to talk for a few minutes. But I already had the feeling that this encounter wasn't going to end well. But the other thing I knew for certain is that I wasn't going to let him dance around my words. I was going to get answers. I was getting ready, applying my makeup and thinking of all my questions I had.

I chose a dress that was appropriate, a purple floral style that was fun and sexy and I picked out some heels to go with it. My hair was curled and done up. I looked in the mirror and I was feeling very confident. When I arrived at his house, he looked me over and I received the opposite reaction from him that I expected. He wasn't impressed with me at all and in fact, he seemed a little irked that I was there. I searched his eyes, looking for a clue of why I got the opposite reaction of what I intended. But I didn't have to look very long. He got right to the point with me.

He said bluntly, "Why are you here?"

I handed him his coffee. He acknowledged the gesture and looked at me. He said, "You look nice, by the way."

But then he repeated, "Why are you here?"

I said, "London, really?"

He said, "No, wait! Why are you still here?"

I knew he wanted an answer, but I wasn't going to give him one because I had questions that I wanted answered.

"Answer my question. I want you to answer my question," he said.

"I know you do, but I think you already know that answer. You know why I'm still here and you know why I can't just walk away," I said.

He looked at me and said, "Look, I can't give you what you want. I don't have time."

I wanted to yell at him and say, "How can you say that, when YOU are what I want!" I wanted to say: "London, you're exactly what I want, and you're what I've been looking for my whole life. You, everything about you, all of you, all of who you are, you're everything I've ever wanted. How can you not see that?"

But in this moment, I couldn't find my voice. I don't know why he had this effect on me. It was like I couldn't verbalize anything. I was in a trance.

I said, "London, look, I want to know why you've changed."

"I told you I don't have time, and I can't give you what you want," he said.

I was about to speak when he said, "Stop. Listen, you are looking for answers and I don't have answers."

He got upset at this point and stood up from the table and leaned against his refrigerator. He started telling me things that didn't make sense to me at the time.

He said, "You're looking for someone to fill this hole you have in your heart."

I said, "No!"

"Listen…" he said. "You're still here because you're holding on to this like it's the last thing that is familiar to you." He started to raise his voice at me and said: "You're here because I am the only person who won't give you what you want."

His words cut me deeply. I wasn't sure on what level he was speaking to me because I didn't quite grasp what he was saying to me, but the pain had already registered in a place that profound.

He said, "Let me ask you something…what would you say this is?"

I said, "Excuse me?"

"Us. What would you call us?" he continued.

I said, "A relationship."

He smirked and said, "This is **not** a relationship."

"A friendship is a relationship," I stated, but I, too, didn't have a name for what we were.

He looked at me and said, "Sylvia, I already told you I don't do labels."

He sat back down at the table, facing me. I had lost touch between my mind and my heart. I was trying to contain myself, but my mind wouldn't respond. I lost my composure. My eyes were so welled up with tears, they just started to spill over, but I couldn't let him see me cry.

I stood up from the table and turned around, but that was as far as I got. My lips were quivering. I was broken down and torn up from the pain of his words. I was crying with no control over my emotions, with no composure, and there was no going back. My heart had to let him see who he was to me, because it was too late.

If he hadn't already noticed, he had shown up too late to this conversation of "us" not having a label because we already had a label, whether he wanted to acknowledge it or not, but it was too late. If he hadn't already noticed, everything was too late!

I'd already fallen in love with him. I'd already invested every emotion in him. In fact, he is my every emotion. It was too late! He'd already fucked me over and over and over again. It was too late! His name was tattooed on every wall of my heart. It's too late. He was the only thing I thought about. It's too late. My soul breathed his name when it said, "London, YOU'RE too late!"

I remember thinking I can't let him see me like this. I barely had time to turn around, but I couldn't move. He came around to me and was in my face. He saw all my emotions and the truth of how I felt for him.

He's too late. Tears streamed down my face. When he finds my face because it's "too late," this had a backward reaction on him. It looked like he wanted to laugh, but I think he was unable to register emotions, and this is what his brain gave him. It didn't matter his reaction because it was too late, and his words had cut deeply.

He said, "I think you need to leave."

My mind registered his words, and as painful as all of this was, I couldn't agree with him more in this moment. I started to walk, but my whole being was shaking. This pain was felt down to my soul. I started walking and I forced myself to stay focused on just that. "Just walk, Sylvia," is what I told myself.

I was so distraught that even this simple, everyday task was an obstacle. I wanted to run. My mind wanted to run away. I felt like throwing up.

I opened the door to my car, and I remember falling into the seat. I was in what appeared to be a drunkenlike state. My mind was in a place it had never been before, somewhere between anger and disbelief and disconnection. I wasn't sure. But the anger took hold. I started to drive, and I wanted to drive into a wall, but really, I wanted to get as far from him as I could, as fast as I could. I ripped my earrings from my ears and my ears started to bleed, but this was good. I was feeling pain somewhere else and the physical pain was so much more warranted and welcome at this time than the emotional pain. This emotional pain was too hurtful. It was too raw. My emotions betrayed me as I came to the realization that it's too late, everything is too late, including saving us.

When we were being physically intimate in the moment, London would say to me, "I want to fuck you." I now see the correlation of the things that were said between us, as they were very literal. Because, in fact, this is exactly what London did. He fucked my body in a way no man ever had. He was violating, intense, dominating, seductive, masculine, rough, provocative, indifferent, and the whole thing made him a mystical creature. But the problem was that he didn't just fuck my body, he fucked my mind. He was stimulating, mentally, and on every level. He kept me intrigued with his mind games. He was seductive, mentally, with his words, but he was completely indifferent, which kept me coming back for more. He fucked my soul. When we found each other this way, it was from literally fucking so hard that we entered into this soul dance. In person, he would whisper in my ear, "I want to fuck you...can I fuck you...will you let me fuck you?" London already knew I had no self-control when it came to him. He already knew my answer to his question and so he did exactly what he verbalized: He literally fucked all of me.

The Artful Mind

To see the divine is to see one in all; it is an unwavering plea in the blurred vision of the madness of this love. It is the determination of the quarrel from within, the search is the beguiling in the enticement of soul to find reason. So I speak words of discord to my soul, for I want to understand the connection, for the element of love surpasses all. The understanding is a plea to the heavens, a dagger in the heart, for it is in the internal knowing, it is of the connection to the divine. Love had pierced through the walls of my heart, but to understand this hole would be to search every piece and element of the flood of emotion…the walls…as to excavate through the layers will be the pureness of truth.

It is like air, and one could not see this, but could feel it. It is with this element of the heart where the connection lay. It is in the underworld of emotion and the afterlife of the soul. It is the tincture in the light of love, where there is no appearance of fear, no doubt, for it is only to see the internal light of truth. It is to understand the truth of soul and how to connect with this truth in the alignment of soul. It is to dare to love with no boundaries.

The element is the transparency of the soul, for all is clear in the highest degree. It is to touch the heart, as the fire is found here like the way one touches the strings of a guitar and plays to the sound of the soul, for the song is one with the Beloved. It is in the art of love, in the art of the residence with all. This is to understand life and make sense of it, a vice of searching oneself, as the heavens are the reward. Fairly it is an illusion of love, truly, a glance, and it is felt in sync with the base of every note of sound, a tone in resonance that nobly awakens the endearments of love's call to the sleeping soul that is likened to the pursuit of rapture, for it is the heart-string with which one is in tune.

When the sounds of the residence of within oscillate to those who awaken home, it is the same sounds of the energy fields of the divine and one opens the mind to the infinite understanding of light. It is the mind's ability to recognize the same radiance of love that lives outside of us, for it is the same love that lives inside of us. It is to find the sequence to see the brilliance of sound and sight come to light, for it is in this space of no separation, as it is all connected in love. It is in the chamber of love, to come in and out like the ebb and flow of life force energy that synchronizes with our breathing. It is the story of life that is told through the art of sound, its illumination with the mind, and in harmony with the soul. One element equates to the other, and so one pushes through the pain of separation in the physical body, for love is light and the connection of light lends to the brilliance of its warmth. It is the warmth of love, for the light sees this love…as this is the same love of the Divine Masculine that lives inside the heart.

As this love flows out, as in the Fibonacci sequence, it radiates with the love that surrounds it and it lines up with linear time, as it is to break through the barrier of time and allow the Masculine energy to find me here in this merge, the contrast; the linear with the cyclic, the feminine with the masculine energy, as it is polarized and then becomes one. It was to be in the time-space reality, as one opens the doors to the heart and to the garden of wonder and walks into its lush beauty of understanding divinity.

In a moment, there exists the enchantment, the act, and the will to seek one's truth in the illusion of love. Fairly every note the heart makes was a step further into the loveliest of sights, the compensation of desires, the affairs of a duet form, the imagination of source and the mystics of all of connection. What does it say, what does it mean, for the element of purity is seen with candor? To sway to the fortune, to yield to the void, for the aptitude is the ray of light that shows over reason. Deceivable to the mind, invisible to the ego, but personable to the soul, as the double-edged sword is the truth that penetrates the measures of desires as the combination of the essences yields a smoldering response.

But the push-pull continues and tests the allies of temperance as it stretches to the depths of the soul to understand the pain. It is to clutch the heart and feel the raw emotion. It is to scream and plea to the divine regarding why the pain, why the unbearable strain, for the succession of the grieving is the truth of the wisdom of the soul. It is not, for to be in this moment is to understand cyclic time, as it comes over me like the Nile River that is my heart, as the exhausted tears turn to blood pouring out. My sight goes blurry and the vision is clear. The pain of the journey would start here in the understanding that hit my mind the same way that London's departure felt in the physical. It was a mourning of his person, a mourning of his past, a mourning of all the memories that we would have to live out together. It is the memory of all of love, for all of time, eternal love and the eternal flame and it would burn me like the fire we made together. It would burn me until my mind could not take it anymore and it would burn me down to the core until I would rise from the ashes once more, like the Phoenix. It was in this time when we would see the other and recognize completely with the eyes of the all-seeing; it would be to know.

Scene XIX

This relationship was taking its toll and I began to question it all. I wanted answers to soothe the pain, but London wouldn't give me answers because he knew what lay in the truth, and that was something that both of us were not ready for, because the relationship had not taken its course. But my heart kept searching him for truth. I needed this truth; however, this long battle over autonomy would reflect through me, hurt me, test me, and emotionally drain me. The most daunting part of all of it was how much I wanted him and how much I loved him. This was put in front of me like a mirror... everything I had worked so hard for, everything I had: my house, my job, my family, my business, my reputation, my life as I knew it… nothing mattered, only him. Why did I feel this way? How could someone have this kind of control over me and this extreme impact on me and my life?

I wanted resolution for my heart at this time. This relationship had become completely illogical, cruel, strenuous, and horrifying. Our texts were so cruel, with the back-and-forth of love and defeat. I would block him and then he would block me. We both wanted to be done, but I needed him to tell me.

I needed to hear it from him, but he wouldn't tell me. He always left a window of hope open, and that is what I held on to because it was all I had. But that would not suffice my heart and I needed him to tell me why he couldn't end it and let me go. He would never tell me, nor give a clue. His emotions and words were completely indifferent.

He was preparing to leave for New Zealand. I texted him one last time.

He said, "Sylvia, why do you want to see me? I'm leaving."

"Do you think 22 days is going to change the way I feel about you? I asked. "Do you want me to wait for you?"

He replied, "Do what makes you happy."

This message was followed by a second text from London: "You can come see me. I'm leaving tomorrow and I have a lot of work, but I can talk to you while I work."

I was wondering if it was because his heart was unsettled. I was wondering if he wanted to resolve it, or if it was for some kind of resolution. I wanted to know what was on his heart more than anything else. I also needed him to know what was on my heart without holding back.

As soon as we saw each other, I could see that look in his eyes, but he was fighting hard on this day. I could sense that he was trying hard to be strong. I could see he wanted to put things to rest before he left.

He walked me to the back part of his house where he has a shop. He told me again how he has a lot to get done but that he would work around me and we could "talk." "Talk" was the magic word and he emphasized it with sarcasm. There was a glimpse of opportunity here; I already knew before this meeting that this would be a time for me to tell him what I needed to say, and what was on my heart. London wouldn't allow me to talk about feelings and he would always stop me before I could say what my heart needed him to hear.

He started working and I watched him as he made the intricate pieces of the gun. All the details that went into it was fascinating. His creativity was amazing. He was fast; he was precise; he knew this skill like it was inborn in him. It was and is his heart's talent; I can see that. It is something he is good at, like an artist. It made me think of his mind and how artistically crafted it is, just like his art of machinery. Every detail was fine-tuned and fitted in the most artistic way. The way in which he crafted his art…there was a place, a perfect spot where each of these metal bits fit perfectly into its spring and each spot where these bits fit was made exact. All the tiny pieces fit into bigger parts, welded to an absolute match for the other. He could look at a bit, a little tiny piece of metal, and eye it and know if it was the right size. This was his art, his natural ability, to make the piece's match, to make everything fit, to make it come together and individually, every piece of machinery he made was unique.

Unique was also the characteristic of his mind and so was his way of thinking, as was every aspect of his thoughts. He had a talented mind, a beautiful mind, a mind that thought differently. It was filled with so much knowledge, so much wisdom, all of it coming together in the most splendid way.

Like the machinery he made, his mind was very fine-tuned. It was its own art form in its ability to process, integrate, and carry out a message.

London was also instinctively intuitive. He had a gift for seeing things, seeing people. He could look at someone and know them. He could look at a situation and understand the thought process that went into the result. What I admired was that he knew his gifts and he didn't question them; he accepted them and used his gifts naturally.

His mind was just like the guns he makes, and his bullets were his words. The power they carried were like the intensity of the bullets being fired from one of his beautifully designed guns. They carried a message that would lodge in the exact spot that was intended. And the message would reignite in the exact place for which it was meant. It was purposeful and precise. His mind had foresight of understanding through otherworldly eyes; his mind was powerful, and his words were its dexterity and force.

I followed him to where he was. I could see that he was busy, but he had taken the time for me and I appreciated his time. I also didn't want to reflect any negativity toward him, because I sincerely missed him and being in his presence made everything better. I wanted to be cheerful. I wanted to be positive. I wanted to keep things light. I missed the fun times between us, and this is where I wanted to be with him today. I didn't know where to start this conversation. He looked up from his machine and said, "So, how is work?"

I thought to myself, "Okay, we can start safe."

I answered, "It's fine, but I feel like I'm just going through the motions."

"Sylvia, why don't you challenge yourself?" he asked.

I said, "I want to."

"Well, why don't you?" he said.

"I'm not sure," I replied.

He said, "That's your problem. You don't know what you want."

I answered, "I do...I just have a lot going on in my life and I feel stuck right now."

That was London's ability to know a situation. He always made me feel transparent in his presence. I wanted to tell him that he didn't know enough about my life to make that observation, but we both knew he was right.

He changed the subject and said, "So, have you started dating anyone?"

"Yes, I'm dating," I said, "and I go out to clubs and meet lots of people, but I'm not into anyone."

"Why not?" he asked.

"Because I can't get into anyone because I'm too much into you," I said. "I got stuck on you, London, and I can't make it go away. I've tried. I've tried and I've tried, but my mind won't stop thinking about you."

He was working over a table and had a piece of metal in his hand. He put it down and turned to me and said, "What is it you like about me so much? What's so special about me?"

I looked him in the eyes because I didn't understand how he didn't understand.

I said, "It's everything about you. It's that you're sexy."

He gave me a strange look when I said this, so I said, "You're so manly. That is what makes you so sexy."

And he said, "I see."

I continued on: "I love your mind. I love your charm. I like how you say anything that's on your mind. I like that you don't care what anyone thinks...you'll say it anyway. I like your confidence. I admire that about you. I love your personality. I love the connection between us, the way you make me feel."

I could see a grin on his face, but he cut me off and said, "You know what you're doing right?"

144

I wasn't sure what he meant, and I said, "What?"

He said, "You're massaging my ego."

I looked at him and had to laugh. I was shaking my head, thinking "that's not the point," but I had to laugh.

I could have gone on and on about all of the things I loved about London if he hadn't cut me off. I had to give him the truth of my heart.

He started going off about something sarcastically and said, "Well, I've already told you that it's time. I don't have the time and I can't give you what you want."

I hung my head because I had heard all his excuses, and I had heard them too many times.

I don't even know where this came from, but I lifted my head to look at him, and my words shot out at him like a dart. I said, "London, I love you!"

He stopped what he was doing, and these words fell onto him and found a place in his soul. I could see the way they shot into him, like a poisoned arrow right through his heart.

I was actually being sarcastic and responding to his sarcasm to me, but these words resonated somewhere deep inside of him. They bypassed his mind and shot him straight in the heart.

I was playing with some bullets he had on his table, and he walked over to where I was and said, "You've been playing with my bullets for a while now. You like those bullets, don't you?"

I was anxious and I needed something to fidget with, but I put the bullets down and turned to face him. I looked into his eyes and I knew he had lost the battle with his ego today.

I said, "Can I hug you?"

He answered and told me that he was sick and that he had been fighting a bad cold.

In my mind, I was thinking, "Do you really think that's going to stop me from your touch or keep me away from you in any way at all?" I don't think he really understood how I felt about him, not if he thought this would stop me from getting to him. I acknowledged that he was telling me it was okay to hug him. I walked over to him and all I wanted to do was hug him, the very feeling of him in my arms was all I wanted. My hands went to his face and I cupped his face in my hands. I took his face and brought it to me, and I looked into his eyes. I put my mouth to his mouth, and we started to kiss. I could taste the antibiotics in his mouth. I could taste the mucous from his cold, but nothing felt more beautiful than this feeling.

We felt the longing I had for him in every ounce of this kiss. The taste was so sensual that it didn't matter what it was. It was his. His smell was rugged, like sweat, but it was perfume to my soul, a stamp of him on my heart.

I was intoxicated in this kiss; his body fluids carried the moment, in any form. His taste, his smell, only added to the ecstasy of the passion and desire I felt for him. As always, our bodies found each other, and we succumbed to the moment.

My hands stayed on his face, guiding him as he kissed my body. My favorite part of this romance was for him to allow me to love him this way. While my hands were on his face, his hands were touching me everywhere. He loved to touch my breasts, and he did. With the passion we felt, I am certain he would have normally ripped my clothes off, but he was being patient. I think we both understood that our time together was coming to an end.

I was wearing high-waisted pants with a corset-style back and he flipped me around and started to unlace my pants. He wanted me to look at him, so he grabbed my chin and turned it to watch him as he pulled the lace strings from each hole by slipping his finger in the middle of each X and pulling it to unlace it. When he got to the last hole, he pulled the entire string and dangled it in my face. He then took the top of the zipper and slowly pulled it down. His eyes were always on mine; he was seducing me with his eyes. He put his hands on both sides of the top of my pants and started to pull them down, and as I watched him do this, I was really wanting him. I wanted to see him, and as if he read my mind, he put his hands in his shorts and pulled himself out.

Every time I saw him, it was always so crude, but in the most arousing way. He is so large, it's almost vulgar, but sex with London was tactful and rough and savage and just naughty. Pure lust, pure excitement, pure pleasure. Everything, he was all of it. He wanted me to see him, he wanted me to look at him, he wanted me to want him.

I needed something; I needed his mouth. So I pulled him close to me to kiss him, but he licked me instead. He wanted something else in this moment; his focus was on this crazy appetite that we have for each other. In my mind, I was wondering how he went from telling me to go out with other guys and how he didn't have time for me, to loving me right then, to the craziness of how much we could love and how deeply we could feel each other in this moment. I looked in his eyes and I saw love, I saw desire, I saw the want and need he had for me. I'm no fool and I knew what I saw in his eyes; his eyes did not deceive me.

One thing I knew for certain, he could not deny me the pleasure, the attraction, the emotion, the lust, the desire, the love he felt for me at this moment; he could not deny me this. He was making sure that I was looking at him. He likes to read my expressions when he makes love to me. He made me follow his eyes and I did, and he looked down and so did I, and I saw him put himself inside me. I closed my eyes with pleasure, but he grabbed my face to bring me back to the moment. I was looking at him and feeling him inside of me. He was studying my expressions as he thrust into me and my head fell back. He grabbed my hair and pulled it. I could feel my brain react to the stimulation, like a tickle on my scalp, but I know he did this because he loves to be in control. He did this again, thrusting harder this time and he pulled my hair harder and then let it go.

He grabbed my hips and pulled me up on the table so that he had a better angle and the position was perfect. His ability to know the exact spot was incredibly precise. When he saw me reach a certain point, he would pull out and try something different. The tactics he used were ever so elusive. It was elegant mockery that heightened the sensitivity of what I felt. It would magnify the experience. I would so often get lost in sex with him, but he would force me back. He would force me to be present in the moment.

He grabbed me by the arms and turned me around. As he picked me up and carried me to his room, I was facing him, staring at his beauty. I wanted to remember all of him, in this moment. I knew this was something different and the ecstasy I felt, this fantasy we had lived together, was coming to an end.

I had to let my mind record this moment for what it was, the feeling for the truth that it was…our truth…and his image of love in my mind. He laid me down on the bed and spread my legs apart gracefully and stood between me.

I could see all of him, right now, in front of me, as he was standing over me and allowing me to take him in. In this moment, and in my memory, he is beautiful, he is large, he is manly. He was—and is—the personified image of masculine beauty. I wanted to be in this moment. I wanted to breathe it in and make every second count.

He took one of my legs and brought it up to his shoulder and he kissed the inside of my thigh. He kept his eyes on me as he reached down and slowly put himself inside me as I watched. He was looking at me and staring into the look of lust, the pleasure he brings to my body.

London reached over and placed my leg back on the bed and pulled me all the way to the edge. Folding my legs up, he placed his hands on the front of my thighs. He couldn't keep still anymore as the rush of hormones overtook us and the pleasure came in powerful, unforgettable waves.

I brought my elbows up and I was still watching him because I was always so mesmerized by the connection we have. My mind was thinking, "Sylvia, live here, stay here, love this, feel this moment, this is yours." This was my every need, my every desire, my every want, right here, right now, loving him, loving me.

My mind wanted to remember this. My heart wanted to melt; my soul wanted to stay here for eternity. I realized I was closing my eyes and my mind forced me to live in this moment, my moment of serenity with him. But now, it's been too long since the last time we were together and the lovemaking was too passionate and the heat was too hot, and he couldn't hold back anymore. He pulled out and he wanted me to turn over. I got into his favorite position and he pulled me up to him and thrust into me hard: once, twice and it was over, as we both reached our state of bliss. He fell on me from behind, both of us breathing hard. His face was against mine. I could feel his hot breath and I said, "I needed that."

He looked at me and didn't say anything back; on that day it was London who had no words. I don't think he understood though, that I literally needed that. I physically craved his body like a drug.

He left for New Zealand and I didn't hear from him.

Spiritual Warfare

Love is everlasting, but with this love affair comes so many obstacles. It feels like a roaring flood that brings with it so much conflicting energy, dark water from a bottomless pit surfacing into a vortex of fierce rage. At this point, it seems like "our story" was meant to unravel here on the earthly realm, but it is not meant for this world, as the energy is too powerful to tame. I feel like a prisoner, captivated by our love, but I would be amidst the tempest of its grip over me. Uncaged emotions seize my mind and bond me to the chase, like a slave captive to its villain of the night. The love itself is powerful beyond me and it is much stronger than me, which feels like a torment, as I am consumed by lust in the eyes of heat and passion, but it is like the scent of a perfume that threatens my sanity. This love is not from the world we know. It does not belong to our reality on the earthly plane, but it comes from somewhere that is beginning to manifest before our eyes.

Like the spark that wakened us to the atom in the cosmos, the effort for self-realization ensues. A battle over my soul is taking place on a supernatural level. It is to understand "the divine man," the heaven that is experienced through London. For in the spark of day, the view of the sum of the heavens is by night. It is to welcome home "love," a love that penetrates the soul and expands beyond the night's gaze. It is the highest love yet. It is the burning of every quality one could experience in the fire, as this is the level where we embark upon on our journey to find answers. This ignition of the flame within me would take a stronghold over my being and on my life. My identity would change at this point…my person, my understanding, and with that, my existence.

As the darkness radiates light, one feels the energy shift, and with it brings about all the vibrations of understanding. For it is the divine, the bringer of all change, like the winds of change that bring in the season. It is divine intervention that brings forth the changed perspective of the journey. It is in the transcendence of the spiritual light, where the gateways of the portals open and connect and the manifestation of light follows, like the synapses in the brain.

It is the time of now, as time is an illusion, for all the realizations of time being that of the subconscious mind bringing forth the perceptive awareness...for it is to understand what this journey means, the darkness that fades into its own essence. It is the transcendence of the worlds and the transmutation of the wounds and the scars...the transgression of all awareness amidst soul understanding for healing. The embrace is from within; it is the eyes of the heart that brings forth the eyes of the soul to see all things for what they are.

Scene XX

I started to realize that it was the first day I met London that the spiritual process of awakening took hold of my whole being: the change, the whirlwind of him, and everything that came with it. There was a particular incident my mind is taken to and it was the day I met him in person, when he had answered my call to the police.

On the day that London had been at my house, night fell, and I was sleeping. I was in my upstairs bedroom and in the middle of the night, I heard noises coming from somewhere in the house downstairs. I was scared, so I waited until the morning to find out what it was. When I went downstairs, I first noticed how hot it was. It felt like I was walking into a sauna. I looked over to the fireplace and saw it was turned on and I realized this was the noise I had heard, of the furnace igniting. I didn't know what to think because the last time the fireplace had been used, it had malfunctioned, and we hadn't used it since. That was Christmastime; it was now July. I wasn't sure what to think. My eyes were drawn to the flames, and I was captivated by its light. I walked over to sit in front of the fire and

I could see in the mist of the flames that there was a message for me, and the message was that I couldn't walk around the fire, I'd have to walk through it. This would be my first initiation to the passage into this other world. I would be playing with fire, a concept that I don't yet comprehend, but its flames were hot and dangerous. This was perceived through my mind.

There was a very strange feeling in the house. From this moment forward, the energy felt like a dark cloud had formed over the top of our house and everyone in the family was being attacked; however, we didn't understand this notion as we had no experience or awareness of this dark side of the mystical realm of spirituality. This was a forbidden concept to me, and I wasn't sure I wanted to explore any part of this notion, but its hidden secrets would soon become part of my story and my existence in this world.

This is when I began to question everything I have ever believed in, everything I had ever been taught, all of my ideas about God and light, my beliefs about good and evil, darkness versus goodness, and righteousness. I pondered the thought, did these two worlds, good and evil, also live side by side? Was this like our senses, an ability to know the difference between right and wrong, what is good and what is bad? It felt like my experiences with London, the way I mirrored him in spirit...was this the same way these two worlds lived, one a parallel of the other, where the spirit world mirrors the physical world?

This concept of spirituality, in fact, is dogma...something that is taught and accepted as truth...words that are told to us about the perceptions of the world from the perspectives of our families and our cultures that have been passed from generation to generation. Is this broader spiritual understanding a space that only few embark upon? The fear of the unknown is manifest in us because we don't want anything to change our preconceived ideas, thoughts, or beliefs of what we believe to be true. I felt all these things. It was scary. It felt like a heaviness that I carried, but it had materialized into my existence.

What was this new energy? It was nothing I had ever known. It was a sensed manifestation of the other side. It was dense, with mystical powers. It felt unsafe and unnatural. It felt like a light source, but something different, something I was afraid to find answers to. But I had embarked to this space by accident and there was no way around it, only through it. The one understanding that everyone knew and felt was that it was about me. There was a whole storm brewing because of me, and I questioned this: Why me, God?

As I was made to accept many realities, this was one that became part of my new world. As was my faith, I understand that it is written that darkness and light exist side by side, so I believed that there must be a reason for all these trials put on my path. As light attracts darkness, I am made to recognize there is something much greater going on around me. I recognized the universe is bringing to me the perfect storm as I entered this world of spiritual taboo, where the whirlwind of this relationship is taking hold.

I sent London a text the next day. I could tell that it was close to the end and I needed him to know something. I said, "London, I have something to tell you."

He said, "Okay, go ahead."

I hesitated at first, but I knew it would be an opportunity to tell him what was on my heart, and I felt like I wouldn't have many more opportunities to speak my truth.

He sent me a text back and said, "Just say what you're going to say!"

He was irritated, I could tell, but I didn't allow this to detour me. I sent a text and said, "Okay, I'm going to tell you…I think I've fallen in love with you."

He texted, "I kind of already knew."

London was true to himself. He was completely indifferent, but my heart needed his heart to hear my truth, even as much as it hurt that he didn't seem to be affected by my love. My emotions, my feelings, didn't seem to matter to him. I started to feel angry at him for not caring, and mad at myself for falling in love with him in the first place.

When London Left

To be separated from our Beloved brings the shadows of the dawn. As we connect deeper into our subconscious mind of understanding, we begin to comprehend what it means to walk in the valley of the shadow of death. Through the memory of the heart, we remember the beginning; we remember true love and wholeness before separation. For in the beginning, the water was separated with the expanse, between the waters, the above "sky" and the below "seas:" separated, but always connected. The connection of the above and below, embodying the spirit and the connection with the emotional body, the memory is that of one, created in the image of Love. As everything is in the balanced state of yin and yang, the black and the white, in perfect harmony, so is the Love in perfect harmony with the cosmos and divine order. The Twin Flame connection is the inner world and the outer world is the connection of true pure love, in complete oneness and equilibrium.

Divine wisdom, the Gnosis, finds our heart in this bond and the higher law comes over our person as does the true nature of the soul, the monarchy of the fluctuation of light energy. It is to go into this aptitude of the process of thought, that of inborn potential of self, to the understanding of life in its full ability and function of innate nature, seen as a whole of the greater whole.

It is to unite body, mind, and spirit into a form of emotion, the connection of soul...an understanding, the tie to the assimilation of divine thought. As we conjure the principles of higher love and higher understanding, it is the raising of the fluency of notion in the vibration of the element of time, as no time and space is the association of the two, for there is no association, only a link in concept.

It is to expand the concentration, to divine the break in this equilibrium, and to venture into the deep. To turn the natural tide of mind and ascertain the limits where there are none and the cognizance is left to explore the realm of what is…with no constraints…but only a rhythm in the beyond of what adapts to the heart's own binaural beats of existence.

It is the miracle tone of healing, as the synchronicity of such a sound in the break of equilibrium opens the mind to astral thought, its natural state when it has not been conditioned. The sound of a natural vortex, the synthesis of energy, a rudimental polarity of the mind, aligned in sequence to the rotation of space and time as one of the other and independent of each other.

It is here I would find my Twin and do the soul dance, the dance of the divine, the element of water; the sound is all around us. The lushness of nature flourishes and grows from the essence of all that is. It is only the soul's light that is seen here in this space and it illuminates all that is around and below. The beauty of life is the only thing that reflects back at us and we look down and admire all that is. We then look back into each other's eyes and see all that exists is through love, the one, single thing that links all else and stands above all else; it is here now. It is crystal-clear…it is magic…it is divine.

We dance in this light; around each other we go, and then we do it again and again and just stare back at the other and there are no words exchanged except the sentiment of divine love, for no words could ever do this justice. It was to see justice in this moment, for all is equal. All is just all; it is divine. It is to be here and allow everything else to fall away. Nothing survives in this space, only the essence of true love, for not even words live here. The cloud of our celestial body merges into the other, and then again and then into each other, and then again. The dance of the Twin soul is the metamorphosis of us; it is here in the transformation, for we transmute this energy… the three elements…as we unify and become one, now in this space.

The Twin Flame concept is an awakening process of enlightenment or an opening to everything, as everything commences from a beginning point, the Virgin Egg. Here we find the understanding of pure matter and sacred geometry, like the flower of life, the lotus, and the magical element of the formation of structure that gives rise to meaning. The Cosmic Egg, the germ that becomes the Universe. It is the element of the third energy, the Third Eye (as written by the spiritualist Madame Blavatsky), like the writer's eye into the field of consciousness, that gives rise to a higher awareness, a higher way of thinking, the connection to the universe and divine thought. It is the linking in the third energy, the eternal and the unknown that is created from union. This initiated the association to the crude energy, the force behind the sexual energy…the third energy…the understanding of the absolute.

Like the works of Nikola Tesla, where he explained it as the transmutation of sexual energy, to the intellect of logic that one could appreciate such insight, both the feminine and masculine energy balance the "abstract" triangle. As it was that decompressed mind that, over lifetimes, the female energy succumbed to a transformation of the mind's philosophy. The Cosmic substance rouses aspiration to be seen as a new idea of design to rise to the occasion of the fertility of one love, as love alone is the symbol of the unity that stands high above all. It served as a counterbalance in the alertness of tender; the infinite and eternal both awaken the mind of suppression and render to supervene the equilibrium after the tempest phase, to bridge the understanding of the divine mind to the baser mind. It was in the power of male dominance the idea of suppressing the sexuality of the female template, to the advantage of using this for creative pioneering.

As Tesla regarded this concept and used his intrinsic, innovative primacy through channeling and visions for the revolutionary contribution to the understanding that energy is cyclic in nature and that the rotating magnetic field is a fundamental principle of physics, and that it defines the use of electrical power. It was mathematics that helped Tesla understand what he was perceiving, the universal mathematics, the formation of numbers, the fundamental numbers to which the universe responds. It was an acute understanding in conjunction with his keen divination skills of vortex math. It was a pattern that he noticed…the three, six, nine pattern of the pyramid… these numbers and the flow of them to a perception of different dimensions like the root of the foundation of esoterics is one; so too, does this root of understanding interlink the numbers.

Tesla found in this work the importance of understanding these numbers' significance, but it would be the connection and interaction of the numbers that gave the greatest significance. It was in the function of math to get clearer insight into the matrix of the universe, as it all started with the flower matrix, the oscillation, a repetitive variation of time, this back and forth to a point of equilibrium.

He noticed a key connection with the numbers three and six, as they served as the other's magnetic field of polarity. Also, he had a second observation and connected further that the number nine existed as an independent number, like a monarch figure. It served additionally to give polarity to the other single digit numbers, on a figure of a circle of the numbers one through nine, as it gives a mirror image to each on either side, also known by some as spin symmetry. Nine represents the beginning and the end of everything and none changing, a consideration of the higher world, the visual of oscillation in a sequence. In physics, the model of reciprocals comes into place, for the symbol of nine as a pyramid of six, nine, three. At each flux field or magnetic field, the parallel lines show the doubling concept and the oscillation field. It is the reciprocal field that always comes back to one, the sheer consideration of energy that gives each number a function, as the numbers are still, but the function that moves and models motion.

In the lower math, you see multiplication, as dividing by any number is the same as its reciprocal, a riddle of math, if you will. In dividing nine, you see that the cross of one, three, six, and nine can cross worlds. It is intelligible as to unify to see the whole of life, through the numbers one and nine; it is to see the beginning of creation or the absolute as the unifying oneness. As this was the story of Twins to understand oneness and its nature, it would mean we would have to meet again at the zero point, the point of creators and destroyers, the center and seed to it all.

To understand sacred geometry and the magic that was the energy of three. It was the third energy, pure love, that would need to be understood from this union. The number three, a spiritual number that gave an initial understanding to vortex math, a funnel of tapping into a third energy: graviton* or chi. This is rendered as the driving force behind creation and is linear, eternal, and base to all.

Numbers one through nine represent the circle. Additionally, all have an underlying pattern, and it is here where you see this enlightenment of competence of association to mysticism. As with a model of sound, all music creates sound, wave vibrations, and color. It was the doubling system into which Tesla was able to tap, that of the energy of motion, translating directly to time and the source of life, as this is the key of creation. It is constantly moving and is the energy of harmonics, the infinite.

This is the spin continuum that the universe takes, the bond of infinity. All matter is in a curved motion; the connection of the female energy coming into contact with the masculine represents the linear energy in the Fibonacci spiral, the golden spiral, and further, the sequence of recurrence relation,** in which one sees mathematic perfection. This was the understanding of the matrix of Twin Flame, the relation and mirror of the other in mathematical context that gives insight of the energy channel, the frequency of higher insight. It was also here where one could see the linear model of communication as to how Twins can always feel each other and communicate by way of this open channel where the signal is sent by one Twin and then it is encoded and transmitted through this channel, and then the receiver, or second Twin, further decodes the intended message

---

*   *Graviton: A hypothetical quantum of gravitational energy, regarded as a particle.*

**   *Recurrence relation: A recurrence relation is an equation that defines a sequence based on a rule that gives the next term as a function of the previous term(s).*

through the third eye. However, one must heed the understanding of blocks where there can be a disruption to this process. This is also an understanding of the connection to the Twin in the 5-D, and the vortex of transmittal energy fields: The Divine Man, the Androgynous, being the sum total.

Scene XXI

When London left, he didn't say goodbye. I sensed I wouldn't hear from him. I thought this break would be good for us, but at the same time, my heart was broken. My mind had a hard time wrapping around the idea of London being gone because I couldn't understand how the connection we had could be so misunderstood. How could he not see it; how could he not want this? It was perplexing because in the moment he was all in…he felt the love, and it was mutual. What was it that changed his mind?

At this time, I started to find some solace in fantasizing about death. The battle going on for my soul was becoming too great. The supernatural energies pulled me in every direction, and I had nowhere to run. My walls came crashing down, and my mind wanted to release. My mind had taken on too much pain. The pain started to set in because I knew this was "for real." He was done, his mind was made up, and he didn't want to see me anymore.

I recognized he wasn't "in" this, but he wasn't being honest with me about it, either. I felt the pull and it hurt. I was so upset, upset with him, mainly, but this carried over, and at this point, I was upset with the world. I was thinking how dare him, how dare he let me fall in love with him, and now that I have, he was treating it (and me) like it was nothing. I wanted to reverse everything and pretend I never met him; I wished I could just replace him. My eyes wanted to unsee what they had seen. My mind wanted to forget his presence in my existence.

I was getting ready for work, and as I was thinking about all of this, I became so distraught. I fell apart and I felt physically ill; I had to call in sick to work. I felt like I wanted to run away, and I did exactly that. I put on my workout clothes and went for a run on the same trail where I first saw him in person. And I ran and ran and ran. I was so angry that the feelings overwhelmed me, and I felt hot tears streaming down my face. I didn't care who saw me crying; I had to release all these emotions. I let out all of the anger, all of the hurt, all the frustration, and I just ran and ran until I was so physically exhausted that when I finally made it home, I fell down on the lawn, in front of my house. I was in the middle of my lawn staring up at the sky and I was angry with God. I said, "God, how can this be? Why did love betray me this way?"

A week passed, and I still didn't hear from London. At this point, I started to get sad and reflected on why he wasn't calling. Was it someone else? Was it me? What is it? My soul wanted the truth. But then I started to look at myself and I wondered, why do I feel this way over someone I met just a few months prior? I reflected on past relationships and past hurt, breakups, and experiences of loss, but nothing ever felt like this pain. This pain was felt on a deep, soul level. It felt deep and suffocating. If I could compare this pain to something, it was like a loss, like losing a physical part of my body, a sort of death, but from the inside.

I was blindsided by this pain because I didn't see it coming. I wanted to hide; I wanted to put my head under my arms and just go away. This is where my mind was, and this was where I turned. In my mind, I could find solace. I could only explain this as a time of terrible tribulations. But I would find my shelter in emotional release. I would find the darkest place I knew such as a corner of my closet, and this is where I would go to pray and release. I would cry in this space: hot, heavy tears of despair and hopelessness. My cry was deep, and there were burning tears of anger coming down my cheeks. This would turn into a tortured cry and then a cry with no more tears, only dryness, a reflection from the inside. My mind knew the only thing left was to let go, but I couldn't. My heart was fighting this battle with everything that it knew. I wasn't ready to let go; I didn't want to let go.

I kept coming back to this place night after night, but my thoughts began to change. They were focused on how I could release myself from this pain, from this hell that I was living. What was it going to take? How could I make it go away? How could I put an end to it all?

The ground beneath me was very shaky and my balance was completely off. I would fantasize about my death. I would think about the best possible option, because this pain was too harsh and unrelenting. Every part of my being couldn't do it anymore. The storm was too strong. It took hold of my life. I had no more control and my emotions were too entangled in this mess of love. The decayed, shattered landscape of my heart was ripped to pieces, defeated, and my heart was left with a gaping hole that was bleeding out.

The pain felt bare, crushing. I would have to hold my heart and I would will this pain away…only nothing took it away and it remained there for me to endure it all. How could this love have this hold on me? It made no sense at all. It wasn't logical. It wasn't natural. It was not real, but it was real. This is when the things going on around me came together in the perfect storm. I would cry so hard that my sobs would become this wet cough and I thought I would choke on my own phlegm and I welcomed the thought. The thought of dying was what took over my mind and the battle from within that had been brewing for a long time came to a boil.

I began to self-destruct in every way you could imagine. I wanted to replace London. I thought it would be easy. What I wanted was a distraction from my distraction to make me forget, to make me stop obsessing over this man. I tried to stop the madness. My mind couldn't take the pain. My heart was feeling so much emptiness, hopelessness, and sorrow. I went through a treacherous low; I wanted to be someone else. I started to change everything about myself: physically, emotionally, mentally. I was so disconnected from myself that I literally wanted to be someone else. I lost myself and then I lost hope. I lost a lot of things. I did things without purpose or care. I started to self-sabotage.

I sought my dark place more often now, and I began to pray, first about him coming back to me, then about taking away the pain. Then I prayed to just make it stop and make all of it go away, and to put an end to all of this. I prayed for the heavens to please save me from this pain and from myself because I just couldn't bear it all anymore. I would say to God, "Save me. Save me from this misery. Save me from this pain. This is an obsession. It feels like sorcery, like a spell has been placed on my soul." It was an illness of a different kind. I had no control over myself or my thoughts. I had no want, other than this man; the addiction was worse than any drug because I couldn't have it and my mind's desire for it was too strong. I couldn't focus on anything. This was an illness, a love addiction. My heart was sick, and I was not healthy. This love had made me ill.

I got a text from London about two weeks after he left. It was the middle of the night and I heard my phone sound and I checked the message. I started reading. It was a message from him. My mind was trying anything to save my heart as I read his text. I could hear my mind's loud and angry voice: "SYLVIA, you already knew this! Sylvia, let it go; let him go!"

My mind was mad at my heart for not understanding what this was before it was too late. My mind started reflecting on the vulnerability in which it was placed. And my mind was questioning my heart: "Why, Sylvia, why, did you offer him all of your being? How could you let him convince you that time was the issue when it was not an issue ever? How could you not see this for what it was? How could you put yourself out there like this? He told you repeatedly, No! NO! NO! Stop! No! You knew what he was saying to you. You knew he didn't want this. Why didn't you protect yourself? You offered him everything, you offered your all, and look at what he did. He turned around just like that and gave it all to someone else. How could you let this happen to yourself?"

My heart had nowhere to turn to, and only pain found it. My head spun with thoughts laced with truth. He didn't want me. My body ached. I'd been in a fetal position for hours now and I just wanted to find peace, but my soul grieved and wanted a release. I came to this dark place for solace usually, but today, I wanted something else. The pain was too great, the emotions too raw, my mind said, "Sylvia, you don't have a choice anymore! Let this go!"

But my heart would say, "No!"

My mind said louder, "You don't have a choice," but my heart stood taller and said, "NO!"

In my closet at this moment, I recognized my mind and heart had completely disconnected. They were in a battle and they had been for a long time, but at this moment, they had stopped communicating. My mind knew what I needed to do, but my heart wouldn't listen. A complete and total disconnect had taken place. I had no harmony, no peace, and this sent me into a bigger mess to try to fight this second battle of conflict going on within myself.

My mind had given up; this love that had taken ahold of my heart was too strong. My mind wanted to release my heart of the wounds as I had come to the realization of how toxic this relationship had become, how the spell overtook me, how the holes in my heart were too big.

I continued to read his message: "I have met someone in New Zealand. I'll be bringing her back with me."

I didn't finish reading the next part of the text because I dropped the phone from my hands. It was as if fifty blades sank into my heart and my heart plummeted to my feet. I put my hand on my chest and I felt the pain, pure excruciating pain. I started to cry…hot tears burning my face. I felt a strong burning sensation in my chest, but I picked up the phone and continued reading: "It was love at first sight…" and the blades twisted, and the gaping hole started bleeding over the open wounds. Blood was pouring out like a river. I threw my phone and I put my hands over my face and cried into my hands, rocking back and forth.

I wanted to give up. I was kneeling with my face in my hands and rocking back and forth, rocking and rocking, and crying and crying.

I started to reflect on the relationship. Why did this dark cloud follow us? At first, it was a lot of drama, and there were things out of our control happening all around us that affected us. The truth was, with all the circumstances, this relationship was never allowed to flourish. It was never given a chance. It was so good, but so bad in some ways at the same time. It was beautiful but horrifying at the same time. The harder I tried to keep things together, to make them work, to make this a real relationship, the more it fell apart. The more I wanted it, the more he pulled away, the more he did this, the more my heart broke because it was too perfect, so my heart bled and bled for this man and now there was no blood left.

Because this is a soul relationship, the pain was felt on a different level, too. The layers were compounded; it was the pain of a deep, open wound that was bleeding out. The anguish, the despair, all the raw emotions were felt on my being. I loved, but I lost, and now I just wanted to be set free of this pain. I wanted to end it all tonight because I could see no other way out from this misery. I felt defeated, but it was more than a gut punch that doubled me over. It was a total knockout, with my body, mind, heart, and my soul knocked unconscious on the floor. My face was buried in my hands and I held my hands over my face as I took what I thought would be my last breath. Then I released myself from the pain as my heart continued to bleed out.

I got to a place where I felt myself being released in the physical. I started to see something. I was startled and confused at first, but then I started to see more clearly, and I recognized it for what it was. I was having a vision, but I was on another plane. I didn't know exactly what this meant, only that my soul wasn't in my body.

An evil spirit with a black-hooded cloak was walking alongside me. I could see us walking down a dark path. I was wearing a cloak myself; it was black, too, and it was also covering my head, flowing all the way down my back. I am hearing a prayer in the background. "As I walk through the valley of death, I will fear no evil, for you are with me; your rod and your staff, they comfort me." I am brought before the gates leading to the abyss. I am here and there is a tangible gate and it has a chain around it, and we stop. I heard a voice. It was loud, very loud, and I was asked in a crystal-clear voice: "Do you understand what you're doing?"

I didn't answer because I was confused. I wasn't fully aware of where I was, where I went, whether I was dreaming, what was happening, and what I was seeing. The voice startled me again and this real vision that I was in became clearer. The voice got louder and more stern. I heard the question repeated to me again: "DO you understand what you are agreeing to?" This time, I couldn't answer because I was trying to focus on what I was seeing, and then I heard clarification, as if someone was reading my thoughts: "You are giving your soul to the Darkness; is this what you want?" I was shaken in the knowledge that this is real…THIS is no illusion…I was standing at the gates of the abyss and I was being asked if I was agreeing to give my soul over to the darkness.

The most distinctive feeling finds me. It felt like I was agreeing to sell my soul as if this was some sort of business contract. I was extremely frightened, and my body shook all over. This is the spiritual warfare going on all around me, a fight for my very soul, and I was giving up in this moment. I was asked again, "Are you agreeing to give your soul to the darkness?" I was being forced to decide right then and there, and this is when I found my voice and I screamed: "NO!!!"

I was released and fell back. I was in a free-fall and I felt an angel catch me. He lifted me up and took me away. I fell asleep from the traumatic experience I had just experienced. When I awoke, my mind instantly remembered, but I wanted to pretend like it wasn't real. I wanted to ignore the experience like I had imagined the entire thing, but this resonated on my soul. There was a clear shift in understanding that this battle was really going on, and it was a battle for my soul.

When I woke up in my closet, I saw a light above me, and my vision came into full focus. I saw the Angel who caught me lay me down and I saw his magnificent wings open. He imbued in me the most peaceful feeling I've ever felt, and he stepped away. When he saw me lift myself up, he began to leave. I will never forget this moment any more than the rest of the journey that was about to unfold, for from this moment forward, everything changed. I was no longer the same. The person I was, my life, this part of my life, everything had shifted. All the spiritual warfare going on around me was understood now.

There was complete disharmony in my soul, and I needed to find answers. This was the moment when the awareness that nothing would be the same ever again came over me. Life was not the same from this moment forward. But I still had to figure all of it out…at home, the spiritual warfare was being felt by everyone in my family with so many strange things happening, and everyone being attacked. I didn't know what to do, or who to turn to for help. I never even believed in any of this stuff. Why was this happening and why was it happening to us?

I would get my answers and they would rain down on me, but first London and I had to complete our connection. We needed to fulfill our journey *with* each other so we could fulfill our journey *through* each other. Through this journey, I would find my God, the creator, obtain a deeper understanding of spirituality and find my answers, the truths of this relationship, and ultimately, I would find myself.

I needed to find truth first. Truth was the hardest thing to deal with, but it would be the very thing that would liberate me. But first, the truth would make me question all things, the things I believed in that I once recognized as truth. My identity and belief system were at the forefront and center of this new reality into which I was stepping.

I entered the spiritual world, almost by accident, but now I understood that nothing is by accident. I know that my book of life had already been written and we are created by a craftsman who perfectly gave us every quality, every attribute, and every aspect of our person and personality. In the same way, He doesn't recognize flaws because these are only qualities that need perfecting. The realization that something in me needed to change, something needed to die…that was what my test was about.

I reflected on this because this is what the bigger picture is…God was telling me I needed to die to myself, to die to my ego. There were too many things that had clouded my vision, but it was only because I allowed these things into my being. I reflected on this, and I saw that there were many things in my life that made no sense. These things no longer served a purpose in my life, and these were the things of which I needed to let go. The things that once worked for me, the things that once were part of me, of my personality, needed to be let go because I was no longer meant to live this way. This experience taught me a hard lesson, and I was now to adapt and change and live my life as a changed, transformed person. I had come to a crossroads in my life and I was made to see things that I didn't want to see or didn't want to face before.

I felt differently after this experience, but I wouldn't understand what had happened to me, not in its entirety, not yet. But that would come soon, as I would become an enlightened soul, and with that would come empowerment and then balance, harmony, peace and joy. And this is how my story would continue to unfold, beyond the bounds of ordinary 3-D reality into the great expanse of true, unconditional love, a pure and supernatural Love that was heaven-sent, heaven-inspired, and heaven-ordained.

I am grateful for this journey and the many lessons it has presented for me to experience, and the many deep lessons to come as I continue my path on the journey to the heart of unconditional love.

EDITOR'S NOTE: Please continue along with Sylvia's journey and be on the lookout for Book Two of "The Enchanted World of Twin Flame."

Reviews

If you enjoyed this book or found it helpful along your journey, please leave a positive review on Amazon, Barnes & Noble, or wherever (or however) you're reading this. We'd also appreciate positive reviews on Goodreads, if you're on that platform. Thank you in advance!

About Sylvia

Sylvia is a popular channeler, Tarot reader, and author specializing in spirituality and Twin Flames with tens of thousands of followers and 2.5 million views on YouTube, as well as thousands on other social media platforms. Sylvia started her career as a nurse, but through the Twin Flame Journey, discovered her talents and passion for spiritual teaching as guided by her trusted guides and Ascended Masters. In her service to Twin Flames, Sylvia's objective is to help people as they break their shackles and ascend the limitations of the ordinary 3-D world to realize their full potential, their  divine essence, and their divine partnerships. She does this by sharing personal stories of her own enlightenment to bring about a greater awareness of spirituality, cosmic love, and cosmic consciousness. The end goal is a better, more joyful, more peaceful, more understanding world, powered by love.

Sylvia invites you to email her at TwinFlameReaders@gmail.com and to please follow her and subscribe to her social media platforms:

YouTube: The Enchanted World of Twin Flame

Facebook: Sylvia Escalante; The Voice of the Divine Masculine

Website: www.TheEnchantedWorldofTwinFlame.com